A Great Gulf Fixed

A Great Gulf Fixed

A STUDY OF THE "GULFS" OF SEPARATION
BETWEEN GOD AND MAN

Justas Iam

Iam/New Harbor Press
1601 Mt Rushmore Rd, Ste 3288
Rapid City, SD 57701
www.netharborpress.com

A Great Gulf Fixed/ Justas Iam —1st ed.

ISBN 978-1-63357-301-7

Contents

Preface

THIS BOOK IS A study of God's employment of the principle of "fixed gulfs". His purpose for the use of "fixed gulfs" is for the maintenance of the separation between His Holy Estate and the sinful estate of fallen mankind. There are several examples of God's ordained acts of separation in the Bible. Some of them are obvious and well-known. Others will be examined that are less obvious, and perhaps uncomprehended by many Christians. This study hopes to show the nature of, the consistency of, and the reasons for, God's employment of "fixed gulfs" between Himself and sinful mankind.

The format of this study is presented in two parts. The literal expression "fixed gulf" only occurs once in Scripture – in Luke, Chapter 16. This is the account where Jesus, reveals the afterlife fates of a poor man named Lazarus and an unnamed rich man. Following that is an examination of some other occurrences in the Bible where God employs assorted types of "fixed gulfs" to govern fallen mankind's access to Him. To support this discussion, various doctrinal points will be offered to document the development of the progressive relationship between God and man. These points are included because of the importance God gives the subject of doctrine in His exhortations to Timothy and Titus by the pen of the apostle Paul. Sound doctrine matters.

1 Tim. 4:13 Till I come, give attendance to reading, to exhortation, to doctrine.

*Tit. 2:1 But **speak thou the things which become sound doctrine:***

Part 2 of this book proceeds to explore the reality of, and the implications of a specific "fixed gulf" that the author labels as the "The Seventh Fixed Gulf – The Fact of, and the Illusion of Free Will". Whether or not the reader agrees with the Scriptural soundness of the conclusions offered regarding "free will", the author's conclusions are not presented in judgment of anyone who maintains a different view. Nevertheless, sound doctrine is the responsibility of every believer and is to be sought.

This be may one reason why 2 Timothy 2:15 warns believers against mis-dividing God's word of truth. It can result in "shame".

*2 Tim. 2:15 Study to shew thyself approved unto God, **a workman that needeth not to be ashamed, rightly dividing the word of truth.***

A careful examination of Scripture reveals how God, through a variety of "fixed gulfs", controls the physical and willful actions of all mankind in any of their self-willed attempts at reconciliation with Him. The author hopes that this book might enhance the reader's appreciation of God's grace in the miracle of salvation, because every salvation is ultimately by *grace alone.*

Introduction

Perhaps you are familiar with the proverbial story about the traveling salesman who gets lost in the country. While standing at a country crossroads, the perplexed salesman sees an old farmer nearby, sitting in a rocking chair on his porch. He approaches the farmer to get directions and asks, "Excuse me sir, do know where the Jones farm is?" "Yep", is the farmer's solitary reply. "Well, is it down this road to the left?" "Nope," replies the farmer. After a few moments of silence, he asks, "Is it to the right then?" Another solitary "Nope" comes from the old farmer. "Okay, so I guess that I'll keep going straight ahead." concludes the frustrated salesman. The farmer shakes his head and chuckles, "Sonny, I hate to tell ya, but ya cain't git there from here. Y'er lost fer sure!"

"You can't get there from here" is a well-worn line in humor, but in the context of getting to heaven, the humor disappears. In the context of salvation, it becomes a serious matter. Unlike the salesman who knows that he is lost, there are a great many people who think they know the way to get to heaven, but they are tragically on the wrong road. To make matters worse, they are unaware of their lost state. If they believe in some sort of heaven at all, they are unwittingly following one of Satan's roadmaps. Satan never ceases working to point people down the wrong road. Millions of people, as a result, are on the road to a destination much worse than the road to nowhere. They are on the road to eternal torment in Hell. Why? Because they have adopted a false doctrine of salvation from either their own, or someone else's, mis-dividing of Scripture.

There are many people whose solution to this potential travel problem is simply the denial of any reality of Heaven or Hell. By their denial, these people excuse themselves of any need to search for the path to heaven. They may avoid any anxiety about "not getting there", but they will spend their eternity in regret. Another fact that such people try to deny, but cannot successfully deny, is the existence of God. Many zealous people try to do so, but try as they will, the Bible calls them fools.

> *Psa. 14:1 The fool hath said in his heart,* **There is** *no God. ...."*

What the "fools" of Psalm 14:1 are actually saying is, "*no*" to God. The words *"there is"* are italicized additions to the original text. When you remove those italics, what the fool has said is "*no*" to God. For a person to know there is a God, which Scripture says that all men inherently know (Rom. 1:19-20), and then to say "*no*" to Him is the ultimate foolish act.

The work of the Holy Spirit, as summarized in John 16, further affirms the foolishness of all denials of God and His righteousness. Notice that the work of the Holy Spirit applies to "*the world*".

> *John 16:8 And when he is come, he* (the Holy Spirit) **will reprove** (convict) **the world** *of sin, and of righteousness, and of judgment:*

Given this truth, the outright rejection by anyone in *"the world"*, of the salvation offer of God through the convicting work of the Holy Spirit is the ultimate unforgivable sin.

> *Mat. 12:31 Wherefore I say unto you, All manner of sin and blasphemy shall be forgiven unto men: but the* **blasphemy against the Holy Ghost shall not be forgiven unto men.**

Scripture pointedly affirms that all men are "without excuse", regarding their awareness of God.

> *Rom. 1:20 For the invisible things of him from the creation of the world are clearly seen,* **being understood by the things that are made,** *even his eternal power and Godhead;* **so that they are without excuse:**

The "seeing" and "understanding" actions cited in this verse are the result of the general calling work of the Holy Spirit among mankind. The evidence of creation is a general call or revelation to all men that a Creator exists. This is the reason why Scripture affirms that it is because of the knowledge of the *"invisible things"* of God that all men are *"without excuse"*. Yet people many still dare to persist in their "foolishness" by saying in their hearts, "....no God".

However, there are many people who are not so foolish or so proud to deny the existence of God. There are probably more people who do believe in an "afterlife" than those who don't. Nevertheless, many of these people are still relying on a wide variety of the beliefs or philosophies of men that will lead them to some presumed sort of heaven. Paul explicitly warned the Colossians against the dangers of the philosophies of men.

Col. 2:8 Beware lest any man spoil you through philosophy and vain deceit, after the tradition of men, after the rudiments of the world, and not after Christ.

The power and impact of the verb *"spoil"* in this verse needs to be understood. It comes from the Greek word "sulagogeo". Similar English translations of this word are "to lead away as booty", or "seduce". Paul's audience in the letter of Colossians were believers. Verse 8 was a vital warning to them about the deadly diversion tactics that Satan employs within the church. However, Satan also uses these same diversions of philosophy, vain deceit, and the traditions of men to keep unbelievers away from God's truth. Satan's prime goal from the beginning is to "sulagogeo" man away from God.

Getting back to the subject of God, while Scripture confirms that all men have an awareness of God, multitudes have lived, and still live, in denial of Him, as noted in this passage of Romans 1:

Rom. 1:21 Because that, when they knew God, they glorified him not as God, neither were thankful; but became vain in their imaginations, and their foolish heart was darkened.
Rom. 1:22 Professing themselves to be wise, they became fools,
Rom. 1:23 And changed the glory of the uncorruptible God into an image made like to corruptible man, and to birds, and fourfooted beasts, and creeping things.
Rom. 1:24 Wherefore God also gave them up to uncleanness through the lusts of their own hearts, to dishonour their own bodies between themselves:

Rom. 1:25 **Who changed the truth of God into a lie, and worshipped and served the creature more than the Creator**, *who is blessed for ever. Amen.*

Many Christians acknowledge the true God and the Heaven where he resides, but even among believers, there is an unfortunate absence of any uniformity of belief about how one gets to heaven. There are many who may actually be depending on the "wrong road" in their presumed journey to heaven.

It is a frustrating thing to take a wrong turn when you are traveling. Worse yet is the aggravation of having traveled for hours down the wrong road before discovering your error. But it will be an error of eternal proportions for those who die and find out that false directions to heaven have deceived them. If they err in their belief about the way of salvation after death, they will join the rich man of Luke 16 on the wrong side of the *"great gulf fixed,"* as taught by Jesus. This *"gulf"* will be the focus of the discussion of Chapter 1. Wrong turns in journeys in this life can usually be re-traced and corrected, but ending up on the wrong side of the *"great gulf fixed"* after death becomes the ultimate "point of no return". The door is forever shut, and the "gulf" is eternally "fixed".

I believe that the phrase *"great gulf fixed"* communicates a biblical principle that much of Christianity has overlooked. Although *"great gulf fixed"* is a phrase that appears only once in the Bible, it is a principle that God repeatedly demonstrates in Scripture. He uses this principle for the same purpose of everything He does – to bring glory to Himself.

Rev. 4:11 **Thou art worthy, O Lord, to receive glory** *and honour and power: for thou hast created all things, and for thy pleasure they are and were created.*

By the use of "fixed gulfs," He is teaching men about the depth of their helplessness in their sin, as well as their utter inability to achieve or assist in their own salvation. The ultimate lesson revealed to men is the magnitude of the truth that salvation is "by grace alone".

"Fixed gulfs" have been imposed by God upon mankind at various times in history to display His sovereignty over His creation. They are acts of God employed to accomplish His ordained purpose among the special part of His creation that bears His image – "man."

The focus of Part 1 of this book is to examine some of the occurrences of the "fixed gulf" principle in Scripture and God's purposes behind them. The repeated occurrences of the "fixed gulfs" that will be discussed, although not labeled as such, accomplish the same purpose as the "fixed gulf" described in the story of Lazarus and the rich man in the gospel of Luke. God is the creator of all "fixed gulfs", and only by His sovereign will and grace can they be bridged. In the account of Lazarus and the rich man, there is a permanency to that gulf, and no hope of crossing remains. The other "fixed gulfs" which occur within mankind's history on earth, serve the purpose of pointing men to the same ultimate and solitary bridge which God will provide by the death, burial and resurrection of Jesus Christ. First, a careful analysis of the Luke passage, which contains the only actual mention of the term "fixed gulf", is needed to establish the principle. The principle will be reviewed and analyzed in the next chapter.

PART 1

The "Fixed Gulfs" in Scripture

CHAPTER 1

The "Great Gulf Fixed" of Luke 16:19-31 Fact or Fiction?

THE WORD OF GOD provides answers to all of the crucial "life" questions that should arise in the minds of men as they begin to use their power of reason, while contemplating their own existence and their surroundings. Questions such as, "Who am I?" "How did this world begin?" "Why am I here?", and "What will happen when I die?", etc. That last question is a big one. Whether or not a man thinks deeply enough to ask any of the other questions, anyone who has any degree of self-perception is most likely to ponder the question about the reality of their afterlife, or after-death, if you will.

I contend that every person, who has any degree of self-awareness, becomes a theologian to some degree when they confront the crucial "afterlife" question. How so? All men are cognizant that life is finite and that death is inevitable. Therefore, they formulate some sort of opinion about their fate after death.

I contend that if people claim to have no other religion or theology, whatever opinion or belief they have about the reality that awaits them after death, is, by default, their theology. Dictionary. com defines the word "theology" as follows: *"The field of study and analysis that treats of God and God's attributes and relations to the universe;.."* Even if a person believes that there is "nothing" after death, that belief is their theology. A belief in "nothing" after death is a belief in the non-existence of God.

Nevertheless, man's Creator has provided the answer to this universal question. For anyone who cares to search, the Bible offers only two possible eternal outcomes for men. Cynics may reply that they don't believe the Scriptures, so therefore the Bible does not apply to them. This view is as foolish as a man who says he doesn't believe in gravity, and therefore it does not apply to him. Whether one believes it or not, the truths of Scripture are as real as gravity. After all, gravity and Scriptural truth are creations of the same person: Jesus Christ (God) (John 1:3)

> *John 1:3 All things were made by him, and without him was not anything made that was made*

The Bible has plenty to say about the universal question about life after death. What will be the state of man's eternal destiny? One of the most specific answers to this question is found in the gospel of Luke, Chapter 16, where Jesus pulled back the curtain to give us a peek at the terrifying fate of two men, each of which resides in one of the two after-life, eternal destinations. In Luke 16: 19-31, we read about the fates of a man named Lazarus and a rich man. Bible critics will attempt to minimize the impact of this account by calling it nothing more than a parable. I will explain below why the label of "parable" is both incorrect and potentially harmful. First, refresh your memory about the revelation of this glimpse into Hell that Jesus gives us.

Luke 16:19 There was a certain rich man, which was clothed in purple and fine linen, and fared sumptuously every day:

Luke 16:20 And there was a certain beggar named Lazarus, which was laid at his gate, full of sores,

Luke 16:21 And desiring to be fed with the crumbs which fell from the rich man's table: moreover the dogs came and licked his sores.

Luke 16:22 And it came to pass, that the beggar died, and was carried by the angels into Abraham's bosom: the rich man also died, and was buried;

Luke 16:23 And in hell he lift up his eyes, being in torments, and seeth Abraham afar off, and Lazarus in his bosom.

Luke 16:24 And he cried and said, Father Abraham, have mercy on me, and send Lazarus, that he may dip the tip of his finger in water, and cool my tongue; for I am tormented in this flame.

Luke 16:25 But Abraham said, Son, remember that thou in thy lifetime receivedst thy good things, and likewise Lazarus evil things: but now he is comforted, and thou art tormented.

*Luke 16:26 And beside all this, between us and you there is **a great gulf fixed**: so that they which would pass from hence to you cannot; neither can they pass to us, that would come from thence.*

Luke 16:27 Then he said, I pray thee therefore, father, that thou wouldest send him to my father's house:

Luke 16:28 For I have five brethren; that he may testify unto them, lest they also come into this

place of torment.
Luke 16:29 Abraham saith unto him, They have
Moses and the prophets; let them hear them.
Luke 16:30 And he said, Nay, father Abraham: but
if one went unto them from the dead, they
will repent.
Luke 16:31 And he said unto him, If they hear not
Moses and the prophets, neither will they be per-
suaded, though one rose from the dead.

You will notice that the phrase "*a great gulf fixed,*" found in verse 26, is highlighted in bold print. It is a truth of God that provides the title of and the focus of this book.

The context of, and purpose for, the parables of Jesus

Before I develop this title, "*a great gulf fixed*", please allow a brief digression about the subject of parables. Stop and think for a moment about the proper classification of the account about Lazarus and the rich man. Many scholars and Christian teachers choose to call this story a parable. But the question to be asked is, "Is it a revelation of a fact or is it merely a metaphor? Wikipedia offers the following as part of their description of the term "parable":

> "A **parable** is a succinct, didactic story, in prose or verse, which illustrates one or more instructive lessons or principles. It differs from a fable in that fables employ animals, plants, inanimate objects, or forces of nature as characters, whereas parables have human characters.[1] A parable is a type of analogy.[2]"

According to the first two sentences of this description, the verses of Luke 16: 19-31 might be appropriately labeled as a parable. This account is a didactic (teaching) story, in prose, that illustrates an instructive lesson about the destiny of both a saved and an unsaved man. Conforming to the description above, it could also be a parable and not a fable, because it contains human characters. But according to the third sentence, this Luke passage fails as a parable because no analogous comparison is offered. It is a revelation about a real place. By this last metric, the Luke passage fails to qualify, according to the Wikipedia criteria, as a parable.

Scripture itself has something to say about the purpose of parables. Read Jesus' explanation for his use of parables. Then ask, is the narrative of the rich man and Lazarus a parable by Jesus' definition?

> Mat. 13:10 And the disciples came, and said unto him, Why speakest thou unto them in parables?
> Mat. 13:11 He answered and said unto them, Because it is given unto you to know the mysteries of the kingdom of heaven, but to them it is not given.
> Mat. 13:12 For whosoever hath, to him shall be given, and he shall have more abundance: but whosoever hath not, from him shall be taken away even that he hath.
> Mat. 13:13 Therefore speak I to **them** in parables: because **they** seeing see not; and hearing **they** hear not, neither do **they** understand.
> Mat. 13:14 And in **them** is fulfilled the prophecy of Esaias, which saith, By hearing ye shall hear, and shall not understand; and seeing ye shall see, and shall not perceive:

The purpose Jesus offered was to hide "the mysteries of the kingdom of heaven" from them for whom it is not prepared. First, ask, "Who are *"them"* and *"they"* that Jesus refers to in verses 10, 11b, 13, and 14?" Verse 15 answers that question.

> *Mat. 13:15 For **this people's** heart is waxed gross, and their ears are dull of hearing, and their eyes they have closed; lest at any time they should see with their eyes, and hear with their ears, and should understand with their heart, and should be converted, and I should heal them.*

Next, it should be asked, "Just who are the "people" Jesus refers to?" The devout Simeon, when he first saw the infant Jesus, confirms that the use of the term *"this people"* refers to the nation of Israel. When Simeon saw the infant Jesus, he declared who this infant would be:

> *Luke 2:28 Then took he him up in his arms, and blessed God, and said,*
> *Luke 2:29 Lord, now lettest thou thy servant depart in peace, according to thy word:*
> *Luke 2:30 For mine eyes have seen thy salvation,*
> *Luke 2:31 Which thou hast prepared before the face of all people;*
> *Luke 2:32 A light to lighten the Gentiles, and the glory of **thy people Israel.***

Notice that the devout Simon, when he spoke of Israel, it was in a distinct context apart from the Gentiles. Only Israel is referred to in the Bible as "the people of God." The church, in contrast, is revealed through Paul as "the body of Christ." These two descriptions are real and distinct labels necessary for any proper exposition of Scripture (dividing of the Word). Israel and "the church" (in Paul's letters) are distinct people groups ministered to by the same Savior. Another helpful contextual understanding is seeing Israel as God's earthly people, while the church (body of Christ) comprises God's heavenly people. But I digress.

To summarize this passage from Matthew 13, Jesus used parables to hide the mysteries of the kingdom of heaven from "them." "Them" = "the people" and "the people" = Israel. But wait, Jesus was speaking to the disciples, and the disciples were part of Israel. A contradiction? No. Jesus' use of parables to reveal truth to the disciples was an example of the divine prerogative that was stated in Deuteronomy 29:29.

You will not find the term, "the people", used in any of Paul's twelve letters to the Gentiles. The only place he uses it is in the letter to the Hebrews, where he uses the phrase "the people" twelve times. In this book, Paul's Hebrew audience knew what was meant by it. I firmly believe Paul authored the book of Hebrews due to his zeal for "the people", who were his *kinsmen according to the flesh*" (see Rom. 9:1-5).

> *Rom. 9:2 That I have great heaviness and continual sorrow in my heart.*
> *Rom. 9:3 For I could wish that myself were accursed from Christ for* **my brethren, my kinsmen according to the flesh:**
> *Rom. 9:4* **Who are Israelites**; *to whom pertaineth the adoption, and the glory, and the covenants, and the giving of the law, and the service of God, and the promises; all, God blessed for ever. Amen.*

Peter, who evangelized to the scattered remnant of Jews, also attests to a letter by Paul to Israel in 2 Pet. 3:15. I believe that Paul's letter to the Hebrews is that letter.

*2 Pet. 3:15 And account that the longsuffering of our Lord is salvation; **even as our beloved brother Paul** also according to the wisdom given unto him **hath written unto you;***

Who is the **"you"** that Peter is referring to in this verse? Below are several references from Peter's epistles that confirm the fact that Peter was addressing Jewish believers.

*1 Pet. 1:1 Peter, an apostle of Jesus Christ, to **the strangers scattered**...*

(In Scripture, Gentiles are never classified as "strangers scattered".)

*1 Pet. 1:18 Forasmuch as ye know that ye were not redeemed with corruptible things, as silver and gold, from your vain conversation **received by tradition from your fathers;***

(The term "fathers" is always a reference to the patriarchs of the Jews. The term would make no sense to Gentiles.)

*1 Pet. 2:5 Ye also, as lively stones, are built up a spiritual house, **an holy priesthood,**...*
*1 Pet. 2:9 But ye are a chosen generation, **a royal priesthood, an holy nation, a peculiar people;***

(In Exodus 19:5-6 Moses prophesied that Israel would be *"a peculiar people," "a kingdom of priests"* and *"a holy nation".*)

1 Pet. 2:12 Having your conversation honest among the Gentiles:

(Here Peter distinguishes his audience from the Gentiles.)

> *1 Pet. 4:3 For the time past of our life may suffice*
> *us to have wrought the will of **the Gentiles**, when*
> *we walked in lasciviousness, lusts, excess of wine,*
> *revellings, banquetings, and abominable idolatries:*
> *1 Pet. 4:4 Wherein they think it strange that **ye** run*
> *not with **them** to the same excess of riot, ...*

(More discriminations by Peter between his Jewish audience and the Gentiles.)

> *2 Pet. 1:4 Whereby are **given unto us** exceeding*
> *great and precious promises:....*

(God never made *exceeding great and precious promises* to the Gentiles.)

> *2 Pet. 2:1 But there were false prophets also among*
> ***the people**, even as there shall be false teachers*
> *among you....*

(Peter's audience would understand the term *the people.*)

> *2 Pet. 3:4 ..for since **the fathers** fell asleep,.....*

In further confirmation of who Peter's audience was, the agreement made at the Council of Jerusalem reveals who the subjects for Peter's subsequent ministry and letters would be. Paul, in his account of this council, acknowledged the separation of ministries.

> *Gal. 2:9 And when James, Cephas,(Peter) and John,*
> *who seemed to be pillars, perceived the grace that*
> *was given unto me, they gave to me and Barnabas*
> *the right hands of fellowship; that we should go to*

the heathen, and they (James, Cephus and John)
unto the circumcision (Israel).

Leaving this digression about the subject of parables, let me proceed with some further reasons why Luke 16:19-31 does not qualify a parable.

First, it is helpful to consider the entire contents of Chapter 16 in Luke. This chapter is an assortment of disconnected teachings from Jesus to the disciples. Verses 1 through 8 are an obvious parable of the unjust steward. There are no proper names used in it. The roles and actions of the "rich man" and the "steward" are a clear teaching analogy regarding the faithful use of what God entrusts to his chosen stewards. The "rich man" is analogous to God, while the unjust steward represents the Pharisees, to whom were entrusted: the riches of the oracles of God, the writings of Moses and the responsibility to open and explain these things to the people. Next, in verses 9 through 13, Jesus sets the context for the purpose of this parable. He explains the importance of, the focus of, and level of, his stewards' faith including the need for the wisdom of living in a world of "unrighteous mammon," and yet remaining qualified to receive "true riches" from heaven. Thus in verse 1 through 13 we read a parable about an "unfaithful steward" and an analogous teaching about the necessity for a steward to be faithful with another man's wealth (mammon).

In verses 14 and 15, we find additional confirmation that this parable is an analogy that casts the Pharisees in the role of the unjust steward. The proof comes from the Pharisees themselves. They took insult from the implications of the parable as being a parable about their deceitful faith in verse 14. Jesus rebukes their self-justifying attitudes in verse 15.

Continuing in Chapter 16, we read some more assorted teachings coming from Jesus. In verses 16 and 17, comes Jesus' teaching about the kingdom of God and the unfailing permanence of the law. In verse 18, Luke records Jesus' clarification about the issue of divorce. These teachings have no necessary connection to the prior verses and are not necessarily chronological to them. Finally, Chapter 16 concludes in verses 19 to 31, where the account of Lazarus and the rich man is revealed. It is here we are given a sobering glimpse into hell.

Starting at verse 19, Luke records a distinct shift of teaching topics. Verse 19 launches into Jesus' revelation about the "afterlife" fate of two types of men –- one is in paradise with Abraham and the other sits condemned in Hell. Because Chapter 16 began with a parable, followed by assorted unrelated, but important teachings, it is understandable why much of Christendom is comfortable in classifying verses 19 to 31 as a parable. The parable of the unjust steward is a critical analogy with a purpose. The otherworldly language of verses 19 to 31 creates the tendency by many to also erroneously categorize this passage as a pictorial metaphor about the state of the departed. But this is a misleading labeling. It is a factual description of the two contrasting, but very real, fates of the departed.

Why? The Bible offers numerous references and warnings concerning the fate of those who die as unbelievers (unsaved) (apart from Christ). If there were no such place as Hell (Hades) (Gehenna), such references and warnings would be deceptive and false. Every teaching about Hell is given to provide a motivation to mankind about the cost of unbelief of the particular gospel (salvation message) which God has revealed in their lifetime. Such warnings provide a part of the foundation and motivation for finding what Proverbs describes as "the beginning of knowledge":

> Prov. 1:7 **The fear of the LORD is the beginning of knowledge:** but fools despise wisdom and instruction.

Any information about Hell, if seriously regarded, should create in men, the fear (respect) of God and His Word. If all the Biblical teachings about the afterlife fate of lost men, including Luke 16:19-31, are either ignored or disbelieved, people will never arrive at the beginning of knowledge because they had no fear of God's warnings to them. Luke 16:19-31 is one of the more terrifying revelations about the reality of Hell.

There is a reason to discuss the question of whether this particular Luke account is a parable or not. It is easier for a person to dismiss abstract parables than to disregard a pointed teaching offered by Jesus. However, the Luke passage is definitely a pointed teaching. It is the only teaching where the inescapability aspect of Hell is specifically revealed. Jesus made this point to show men the eternal irrevocability of the afterlife judgment for unbelief. This teaching is as factual as the truth of John 14:6, where Jesus unequivocally states that He is *"the way, the truth and the life"*.

Below are some additional arguments against the Luke 16 passage being a parable as found on the website of The Middletown Bible Church, Middletown, CT. They contend:

> *"You will notice that the Lord did not say that it was a parable. Even if it were a parable, it would indeed be a unique parable for the following reasons:*

> 1. *It would be the only parable in the Bible that describes certain things that are outside of the realm of human experience. All the other parables talk about things that we are familiar with such as birds, seed, fields, pearls, wheat, barns, leaven, fish, etc. (see Matthew 13, etc.). This passage is different because it talks about what happens to two men after death, and this is a realm where none of us have had any personal experience. A parable is an earthly story with a heavenly or spiritual significance but Luke 16 transcends the realm of the earthly.*

2. *It would be the only parable in the Bible that uses a proper name (Lazarus).*

3. *It would be the only parable in the Bible that makes mention repeatedly of a historical person--Abraham. Moreover, this historical person actually carries on a dialogue with the rich man! Indeed, mention is also made in this parable of Moses, another historical character. What other parable speaks of real, historical persons?*

4. *It would be the only parable in the Bible that describes the places where the dead go (Hades, Abraham's bosom, a place of torment).*

5. *It would be the only parable in the Bible that makes mention of angels. Compare Matthew 13 verses 24-30, 36-43, 47-49 where angels are mentioned in the explanation of the parable but not in the parable itself.*

6. *If Hades is not really a place of torment then this would be the only parable in the Bible where the Lord Jesus taught error instead of truth. GOD FORBID!"*

I would add some observations to this list from the Middletown Bible Church.

1. Again, I reference Matthew 13:11, where Jesus reveals the reason for teaching by parables.

   Mat. 13:10 And the disciples came, and said unto him, Why speakest thou unto them in parables?
   Mat. 13:11 He answered and said unto them, Be-cause **it is given unto you to know the mysteries of the kingdom of heaven, but to them it is not given.**

   But, in contrast to the explanation given in verse 11 above, in verses 19 to 31 of Luke 16, Jesus is not revealing a "mys-tery of the kingdom of heaven. The kingdom of heaven, which is mentioned only in Matthew's gospel, is a promised earthly kingdom that is but one part of the kingdom of God. Luke 16:19-31 is not a parable about the kingdom of heaven. It is uncovering a hidden truth about the afterlife reality that is part of the kingdom of God, about which both Jews and Gentiles need to know.

2. It is worth noting that the actual name of the man in Paradise (Abraham's bosom), is mentioned - Lazarus. In contrast, the name of the rich man in hell is not given. It seems correlate with the personal relationship Christ will have with all saved humanity and the future disavowal by Christ, at the judgment of all unbelievers, when Jesus will say *"...I never knew you, depart from me..."* (Matt 7:23) before He condemns them to hell.

3. Jesus' narrative of the rich man and Lazarus confirms two afterlife realities. Those realities are the fact that there are only two alternative experiences available for all departed souls. Jesus affirms this in John 5:29. Note the word *"all"*.

*John 5:28 Marvel not at this: for the hour is coming, in the which **all** that are in the graves shall hear his voice,*
*John 5:29 And **shall come forth; they that have done good, unto the resurrection of life; and they that have done evil, unto the resurrection of damnation.***

4. Jesus also reveals four, previously unknown facts about these two eternal destinies, which are of great importance to men.

a. The torments are as real to the rich man as if he were physically in hell, as evidenced by his pleadings for a type of physical relief from father Abraham – a drop of water. While the comfort of Lazarus will be, I believe, the ultimate *"peace that passes all understanding"* that Paul mentions in Philippians 4:7. Both conditions will be factual, physical experiences of the souls of men after death.

b. It also bears notice that the tormented rich man never asks for forgiveness for the sins that put him where he is. His immediate focus was his desire for physical relief for his sufferings. He is fully aware that the window of opportunity for forgiveness has closed.

c. There is no available access or path of transport by any action of those who reside on either side of the *"great gulf"*; to those in torment, who desire to reach the state of comfort in paradise, or to those in comfort which might want to give relief to those in torment. The phrase in Luke 16:26, where Abraham, responding to the rich man, says *"....so that they which would pass from hence to you cannot."* is very interesting. It seems to indicate the possibility of awareness by those in comfort of those who are not; hence, there could arise a natural desire to want to offer them some relief. I don't know if this awareness will continue in heaven, but alas, the great gulf is eternally fixed by the judge of all mankind so that no passage in either direction is permitted. If such awareness should continue, it will serve to magnify the value of saving grace to every recipient of it. Every saved person would realize, "There, but for the grace of God, go I."

d. A further profound revelation must be noted about the response of the rich man to his plight. When no personal relief was allowed to the rich man, his concern turned to his five brothers. He asked for a special evangelistic effort to be made to prevent their fall into the same fate as he received. But he was informed that his brothers have all the information they need to avoid the same fate.

5. All of the parables that Jesus offers are accompanied by His explanation of the analogy for the sake of His intended audience. To the account of Lazarus and the rich man, no follow-up analogy is offered nor needed. The facts of the account explain themselves. If believed, these facts should terrify men.

6. Finally, although the earthly ministry of Jesus was confined to the Jews and the particular content of Luke 16 is addressed to a Jewish audience, the truths revealed by verses 19 to 31 are not exclusive to Jews. The Gospels, though written in a Jewish context, by and about a people still under the Law, do contain some principles and truths coming from Jesus during His earthly ministry that apply to all humanity. This glimpse of the reality of Hell and Paradise is one such truth offered as a sobering warning to all men. The finality of Hell is no myth and it makes no distinction among men, Jew or Gentile.

The Mystery of "Understanding"

Thus, in a narrow sense, parables themselves are a type of "fixed gulf" that Jesus uses to block the understanding of a certain truth by a certain audience – unbelieving Jews. As stated in Matthew 13: 13-14, the "fixed gulf" purpose of parables was in fulfillment of prophecy. Non-believing Jews were blocked from comprehending parables by the use of their sight, hearing or understanding.

How was their understanding prevented? A generally over-looked truth of Scripture is the fact that God/Jesus controls the understanding of men. The lack of men's understanding was prophesied. Referring again to the 13th chapter of Matthew, after the disciples asked him why he taught in parables and Jesus defined the limits of the intended audience, His next answer revealed the reason behind the controlling of the understanding of unbelieving Israel.

> *Mat 13:13 Therefore speak **I to them in parables**: because they seeing see not; and hearing they hear not, neither do they understand.*
> *Mat 13:14 And **in them is fulfilled the prophecy of Esaias**, which saith, By hearing ye shall hear, and shall not understand; and seeing ye shall see, and shall not perceive:*

This announcement by Jesus wasn't a prediction. It was a prophecy fulfilled. God caused their lack of understanding. He applied the same veil of understanding upon the 12 disciples when Jesus foretold them of His pending crucifixion. They did not, and could not, believe Him because Jesus openly states that God hid their understanding of His spoken words.

> *Luke 18:34 And **they understood none of these things**: and **this saying was hid from them**, neither knew they the things which were spoken*

It would be a logical question to ask, "How it is fair for God to hide things from some men?" It is fair because God is sovereign, and He does as He wills. As the book of Daniel points out, this is a question man does not get to ask of his creator.

*Dan. 4:35 And all the inhabitants of the earth are reputed as nothing: and he doeth according to his will in the army of heaven, and among the inhabitants of the earth: and **none can** stay his hand, or **say unto him, What doest thou?***

Thus, God has the privilege of both keeping (hiding) secrets, and of revealing them when, and to whom, He chooses. By the use of parables during His earthly ministry, Jesus was purposely creating "gulfs" that blocked the understanding of certain people. His secrets and his revealing of secrets are both done according to God's divine and immutable purposes.

*Deut. 29:29 The **secret things belong unto the LORD our God**: but those things which are revealed belong unto us and to our children for ever, that we may do all the words of this law.*

The explanation for parables is that they *"belong (are given)"*, to the children of God. This is the reason why it is important that the account of Lazarus and the rich man not be treated as a parable. Jesus was unlocking a crucial secret revealed for all men. It was a clear revelation from Jesus about the reality of hell.

The word translated "hell" appears 31 times in the Old Testament and 23 times in the New. It is not a neglected topic in Scripture. The threat of hell was never intended to be a mystery to men. The many mentions of hell in Scripture are intended to engender the concept of the "fear of God" in men. The account of Lazarus and the rich man should be a sobering warning to any reader. No interpretation is necessary. For this reason, the label "parable" is an improper description of Luke 16:19-31 account.

CHAPTER 2

The "Fixed Gulf" Principle in a Broader Context

IF YOU ENJOY SPY and mystery novels as I do, then you enjoy intricate plots and surprise endings. When reading novels, you often find yourself speculating about what will happen next. You ask yourself, "Where is this plot is going?" and "How is it all going to end?" However, while the author wants his readers to ask these questions, the author knows the answers to these speculations. Reading the Bible from start to finish is a comparable experience. First-time Bible readers may have the same speculations. After Adam and Eve were banished from their paradise life in the Garden of Eden by their creator, a first-time reader would naturally wonder, "now what?"

As the author of the Bible, God knows the purpose and the end of the story. Also, like a good mystery writer, God does not reveal his entire plot at once. He progressively unfolds the history of the focal point of the story, man, made in God's image.

But, unlike the mystery novels written by men, God, as the author, has a role in His mystery. In human novels, as characters are introduced into the narrative and events happen, we are led to wonder about the various roles they will play in the narrative. In the biblical narrative, God often appears as a participant. His "in time" interactions with men can easily lead to confusion in the reader's mind about God's role. This confusion arises from the natural tendency of the reader to view God as a character with finite knowledge and emotions on the same level as man, because of the way the narrative flows. For example, as the book of Genesis unfolds, God was clearly defined as the creator of everything. As such, by His authority, God expels Adam and Eve from the Garden of Eden for their disobedience. Then, as men try to live by their consciences, they degenerate morally to such a degree that we read the following in Chapter 6:

> Gen 6:5 And **GOD saw** that the wickedness of man was great in the earth, and that every imagination of the thoughts of his heart was only evil continually.
> Gen 6:6 And **it repented the LORD** that he had made man on the earth, and **it grieved him at his heart.**

These verses give us the picture of God, as a spectator of His creation, and regretting His act of creating man to the point of being "grieved" about it. God "saw", "repented" and was "grieved". By this language, God is virtually humanized as having done something He wishes He had not done and thereby causing Himself actual grief.

The description of His reactions to the moral decay of the crown jewel of His creation – man – created in His image, appears incompatible with God's attributes of omniscience and omnipotence. As an omniscient God, He cannot learn anything new. Yet, these verses portray God as having observed the outcome of an experiment that has failed and reacted in grief. Now, in his grief, it seems as though God must move to the proverbial "plan B". How does this narrative align with the truth of Acts 15:18?

Acts 15:18 **Known unto God are all his works from the beginning of the world.**

This verse tells us that God knew about what He saw in Genesis 6:5, before it happened. So why would He react as being repentant and grieved for this outcome of man's moral degeneration? All of the basic human emotions (except for fear) found in man are also in God, who is the image pattern for man. An alert critic may ask, "What about hate?" the answer is simple. God hates sin.

The attributes of omniscience and omnipotence are also fully part of God, but these are not attributes found in man. A profound truth about Christ, who is the bodily image of God, is that He is fully God and fully man. This truth taxes the finite limits of our comprehension as humans, but it is a truth that does not allow us to put limits on God when we read of His responses, such as in Genesis 6:6. God foreknew the situation of Genesis 6:5, yet it still repented and grieved Him.

Remember, the mystery novels written by men, are fiction, while the progressive revelation of the mystery of the Bible is nonfictional truth, coming from the Creator God, who also happens to have an interactive role in the narrative of His own story. Where God seems to react to events, it must be remembered that He is also the author of the story.

God's use of "fixed gulfs" represents just one aspect of how He intervenes in His interactions with man. In this book, the purpose is to examine what I submit are some wider applications of the expression, *"a great gulf fixed"* in Luke 16. "Fixed gulfs" are the theme to be developed in the proposition about a subtle, but factual principle, that is foundational to all of God's interactions with all mankind.

In preparation for this examination, there are three critical Biblical truths that must be believed by the reader. If these truths are not accepted literally, as Scripture presents them, then any further discussion is irrelevant. My arguments will have no basis of support if these truths are not believed.

The first truth is the context that covers all scripture, as offered in 2 Timothy 3:16. If this is a lie, then man can parse the Scriptures and interpret them as he pleases without repercussions. Scripture can mean whatever the reader desires.

> *2 Tim. 3:16 **All scripture** is given by inspiration of God, and is profitable for doctrine, for reproof, for correction, for instruction in righteousness:*

This verse does not allow for tampering with God's Word. Second, is the truth of Genesis 1:1. If this is not true, then you, the reader, must still be looking for some other, totally credible, and demonstrable explanation for the existence of this amazing universe. Evolutionary theory is desperate fiction. Scientists on this little dot in the universe have electronically searched the heavens in vain for any evidence of the existence of some other form of intelligent life, such as ours. Where is it? All they hear is the silence of God. If they could hear God's opinion of their efforts, this is what they would, and will, hear.

> *Psa. 2:4 **He that sitteth in the heavens shall laugh: the Lord shall have them in derision.***

In contrast, however, the existence of creation, as explained by God, had a beginning and will have an end. It is the work of a sovereign God who is without beginning or end. This explanation of the universe has no loose ends. This verse concisely states where we, and the creation around us, came from.

> Gen.1:1 **In the beginning God created the heaven and the earth.**

The third critical, foundational truth is the truth just quoted from Acts 15:18. The concept of an eternal, omniscient God is beyond the scope of man's finite comprehension abilities. From God 's perspective, it is not that He does not know what He "will do". It is the truth that God knows what He has already done, from beginning to end.

> Acts 15:18 **Known unto God are all his works** *from the beginning of the world.*

The Old Testament corollary that affirms Acts 15:18 is found in the prophecy of Isaiah.

> Isa. 46:10 **Declaring the end from the beginning,** *and from ancient times the things that are not yet done, saying,* **My counsel shall stand, and I will do all my pleasure:**

Standing on the foundational truths of these verses, we need to track the history of God's relationship with mankind to see the development of, and the implication of *"a great gulf fixed"*. Although this little phrase only appears in the Luke 16 passage of Scripture, I suggest that it is a principle that God repeatedly applies in the unfolding history of man's relationship with Him, until the only possible bridge over this gulf, His Son, Jesus Christ, is revealed. One might point to the fact that there is no such bridge in Luke 16: 19-31. The absence of any "the bridge" in this account, as Jesus tells it, is one of the central teaching points He is making.

Once the bridge has been revealed and rejected by any man on earth, there is no further bridge(s) available. In hell, "the bridge" is gone. All that remains is the *"great gulf fixed"* for all eternity.

Note again, that the tormented rich man was not looking for the bridge in hell. It tells me that he did not dispute his fate. He only wanted two things – the relief of a drop of water and a warning sent to his brothers. (This refutes the adage that says, "misery loves company") Read again, the rich man's last appeal made for his brothers.

> *Luke 16:27 Then he* (the rich man) *said, I pray thee therefore, father, that thou wouldest send him (* Lazarus*) to my father's house:*
> *Luke 16:28 For I have five brethren; that he may testify unto them, lest they also come into this place of torment.*
> *Luke 16:29 Abraham saith unto him, They have Moses and the prophets; let them hear them.*
> *Luke 16:30 And he said, Nay, father Abraham: but if one went unto them from the dead, they will repent.*
> *Luke 16:31 And he said unto him, **If they hear not Moses and the prophets, neither will they be persuaded, though one rose from the dead.***

If you know much about the Bible at all, there is an irony of the beggar man in this account being named Lazarus. The truth of Abraham's last response to the rich man in verse 31 above is reinforced by the fact that earlier, Jesus, in His earthly ministry, raised a different man from death, whose name also happened to be Lazarus. The result of this miracle, done in real-time and space, done before the eyes of living men, was that only some of the eyewitnesses believed in Jesus. This miracle did not impact the Pharisees. They not only remained in unbelief, but they became increasingly intent on removing Jesus from their world. Later, we learn that some Jews were as interested to see Lazarus, because of his return from the grave, as they were to see Jesus (John 12:29).

Nevertheless, the John 11 account of Jesus calling Lazarus from the grave and its effect upon the witnesses of it, corroborates Abraham's response in Luke 16:31. The sending of, or appearance of, one from the grave will not guarantee saving faith in those still living. Paul confirms the same truth in 1 Corinthians 15, where he affirms the visual appearance of Christ to many people after His death, burial, and resurrection. It did not accomplish universal belief. At the Council of Jerusalem, Paul reminds the Council of the multiple sightings of the resurrected Christ.

> *1 Cor. 15:5 And that* **he was seen of Cephas** (Peter)**, then of the twelve:**
> *1 Cor. 15:6* **After that, he was seen of above five hundred brethren at once;** *of whom the greater part remain unto this present, but some are fallen asleep.*
> *1 Cor. 15:7* **After that, he was seen of James** (the leader of the council and the brother of Christ)**; then of all the apostles.**
> *1 Cor. 15:8* **And last of all he was seen of me** (Paul) **also,** *as of one born out of due time.*

If faith came by "seeing", Jesus could have remained on earth and dispensed salvation to all who would "see" Him. But, faith does not come by mere sight. It comes only by hearing which, in turn, only comes "**by**" the word of God. (Rom. 10:17).

*Rom. 10:17 So then **faith cometh by hearing, and hearing by the word of God.***

The real truth Abraham is relating to the rich man in Luke 16, is that the bridge of salvation has been prophesied and provided to all men in their lifetime. After death, there will be no other offers of salvation made to men. In the remainder of this book, I propose that, in a broader view of the "fixed (un-crossable) gulf" principle, we see that it is an action used by God in His sovereign interactions with both unbelievers and believers. If we examine the Scriptures and the history of God's interactions with mankind, this "fixed gulf" principle, in the context of any achievability of salvation by any efforts of man, will emerge.

Let's look through the Scriptures to see if this argument has merit. The next six chapters will cite some examples of God-created "fixed gulfs" that both overtly, and sometimes subtly, reveal man's helplessness to gain salvation by their own efforts. Like the "gulf" that confronted the rich man in hell, three of the six "gulfs",discussed in the following chapters, are clearly discernable. They are distinct interventions of God that deny men any "free will" access to Him. Meanwhile, the other three gulfs are not immediately apparent as salvation barriers, but yet, they are still God-created, real "fixed gulfs" that prevent any person from having a causative role in his or her salvation. These types of "gulfs" can be discovered by careful, rightly divided, Bible study.

Both types of "gulfs", the obvious ones and the less-than-obvious, or subtle types, are equally beyond the reach of any man's immediate, personal ability to have an initiating role in their salvation. God controls all passages across His "gulfs". Only God can allow and cause the passage of any individual across a gulf He has created. All of these gulfs demonstrate and support the Biblical truth that Jonah proclaimed. These verses affirm that salvation is not a co-operative accomplishment of God and man.

> *Jon. 2:9 But I will sacrifice unto thee with the voice of thanksgiving; I will pay that that I have vowed.* **Salvation is of the LORD.**

Salvation belongs entirely to the Lord and the bestowal of salvation (mercy) upon "whom He will", also belongs to Him.

> *Rom. 9:18 Therefore hath he mercy* **on whom he will** *have mercy, and* **whom he will** *he hardeneth.*

This verse irritates many Christians because it seems to put God in an arbitrary and unfair light. These accusations are easily answered when one acknowledges these two facts of creation. One is that, at creation, all men were "in Adam" (Rom. 5:12) and two, that God did not create man in a "hardened state". Genesis tells us that everything God created was pronounced "good". Man (all men) is solely responsible for his own sin. All subsequent "hardening" work by God is an act upon an already willfully rebellious and sinful heart.

Having established the premise of the principle of God's sovereign control of, and use of, "fixed gulfs", the remainder of this book will proceed to reveal and examine several occurrences of this principle in Scripture.

CHAPTER 3

The "fixed gulf" in Eden

THE CREATION ACCOUNT OFFERS a perfect example of the confusion that exists among Bible readers who do not understand the dual roles of God in Scripture. Like the point made in the last chapter, God is both the author of all of Scripture (2 Tim. 3:16) and a participant in the account of His historical interactions with humanity. Despite God's conversations "in time" with men, He is always sovereign and never "locked in time" like man, even though the Biblical narrative, at times, seems to portray God as being at the mercy of the actions of men, causing Him to adjust His plans. Chapter 1 of Genesis gives us the initial details of the creation of heaven, earth, plants, animals, and man. Genesis 1:28 records God's instructions as He commands Adam to have dominion over the new creation. Chapter 2 follows up with more details about His creation, including God's instructions as He commands Adam to have dominion over the new creation.

*Gen. 1:28 And God blessed them, and God said unto them, Be fruitful, and multiply, and replenish the earth, and subdue it: <u>and **have dominion** over the fish of the sea, and over the fowl of the air, and over every living thing that moveth upon the earth.</u>*

Then, in Chapter 3 Satan enters the story. Many readers, at this point in the narrative, fail to ask, "Where did Satan come from?" and "When was Satan created?" Allow the author a short digression to ponder some "mystery" questions about Satan. Scattered through the Bible there are assorted verses that give us information regarding Satan. From the verses below we learn the following facts about Satan:

1. He was created and as a creation of God he was perfect in wisdom, beauty and all his ways, i.e. sinless. Ezek. 28:12-15 (All of God's creations were "good" Gen.1:31)
2. He was the "anointed cherub" Ezek. 28:14
3. As an angel, he had an original estate (place) Jude 1:6
4. This estate is described as: Eden, the garden of God. Ezek 28:13; the holy mountain of God, where he walked amidst "stones of fire". Ezek. 28:14;
5. He was cast "down" from heaven. Luke 10:18; and to the ground. Ezek. 28:17; 2 Peter 2:4 (The implication is that Heaven is "up".)
6. His pride was the source of his fall. Ezek. 28:17; perhaps Isa. 14:13-14
7. His nature as a "murderer" and the "father of lies" happened at "the beginning". John 8:44

When Satan deceived and tempted Eve and Adam into disobedience, the spiritual realm shuddered. It necessitated the creation of a gulf of separation because God could not have fellowship with sin and sinners in the same manner as His fellowship had been with sinless man, whom God created. God's judgment was pronounced upon Adam, upon Eve, upon all of creation and upon the serpent. This judgment was followed by the banishment of the man and woman from Eden, and it was enforced by a permanent blockage of the entrance of the garden, guarded by Cherubims and a flaming sword.

> *Gen. 3:22 And the LORD God said, Behold, the man is become as one of us, to know good and evil: and now,* **lest he put forth his hand, and take also of the tree of life, and eat, and live for ever:** *Gen. 3:23 Therefore the LORD God sent him forth from the garden of Eden, to till the ground from whence he was taken. Gen. 3:24* **So he drove out the man; and he placed at the east of the garden of Eden Cherubims, and a flaming sword which turned every way, to keep the way of the tree of life.**

This passage describes the first "fixed gulf" within creation. This gulf was as obvious and impassable as the gulf described in Luke 16. The reason for the banishment is stated in verse 22. The expression "*...lest he put forth his hand and take....*" is indicative of the foreknowledge of the Godhead about the potential action of fallen mankind that could have allowed them to obtain eternal life by their own wills. The underlined part of verse 22 is essentially saying, "We cannot allow a man to save himself." Among other reasons why a man can never be allowed to save himself, or even have an independent role in saving himself, is the sovereignty of God. If man could save himself, then it would mean that man has power over his sin; that he was not sin's captive. It would reinforce a god-like status in the mind of man by his willful control over his own existence. If a man performs even an iota of independent work in his salvation, God's sovereignty is disparaged. The very idea of disparaged sovereignty is antithetical. By allowing the insertion of any "independent" work of man into his salvation, it makes the declaration of Jonah about salvation, at best, a half-truth.

> *Jonah 2:9 But I will sacrifice unto thee with the voice of thanksgiving; I will pay that that I have vowed.* <u>*Salvation is of the LORD.*</u>

What must be remembered by the reader from this sequence of events in Eden is that this is not the beginning of a cosmic game of checkers where God makes a move, then man makes a move, then God makes a counter-move, etc. If it is *"known to God from the beginning are all His works"*, then He certainly knows every deed and action of man. He is not just a character in the story, which merely acts and reacts. God is both in the story and over it. The Scriptures not only give us the account of man's history and his ever-changing relationship with God, but they also provide a progressive revelation of who God is. The ultimate depth of the truth of *"Salvation is of the Lord"* will be revealed through the repeated applications of the divine principle of God's "fixed gulfs". Because God is the one who creates any and every "fixed gulf", only God can be the one who can save His elect from the bondage of their separation from Him. He is sovereign over the "fixed gulfs" that He creates.

Someone might ask the question, "Why didn't God just rectify the sin problem and the resulting breach of separation immediately?" It is a reasonable question. I offer two reasons. First, as the Biblical narrative unfolds, man must learn about God's omnipotence, His omniscience, and His omnipresence. It is a long lesson. The ultimate lessons that man must learn concerning the attributes of God are: the love of God and the grace of God. The Apostle John concisely identified the essence of God, which is love.

> *1 Jn. 4:7 Beloved, let us love one another: for __love is__*
> *__of God__; and every one that loveth is born of God, and*
> *knoweth God. 1 Jn. 4:8 He that loveth not knoweth*
> *not God; for __God is love__.*

In the New Testament, we learn that the apostle Paul was the minister of the dispensation of grace,

> *Eph. 3:2 If ye have heard of __the dispensation of the__*
> *__grace of God which is given me to you- ward:__*

Throughout the 13 books that Paul authored by divine inspiration, the love of, and grace of God are continually stressed. Here is one example.

> *2 Cor. 13:14 __The grace of the Lord Jesus Christ,__*
> *__and the love of God, and the communion of the__*
> *__Holy Ghost, be with you all__. Amen*

This verse reveals the Trinitarian truth about God along with the fundamental essences of God: "love" and "grace". To reveal all of God's attributes He ordains the unfolding of the expanse of history, as revealed in the Bible and as continued to this day.

The Mystery of Election

The second part of the reason He did not "fix" things right away, was not revealed until deep into the New Testament, where Jesus revealed, through Paul, the mystery of election. Scripture reveals this mystery as having been done, not "*in the beginning*", but "*before the foundation of the world.*"

> *Eph. 1:4 According as __he hath chosen us in him be-__*
> *__fore the foundation of the world__, that we should be*
> *holy and without blame before him in love:*

2 Thess. 2:13 But we are bound to give thanks alway to God for you, brethren beloved of the Lord, because **God hath from the beginning chosen you to salvation** *through sanctification of the Spirit and belief of the truth:*

The electing work of God is one of the few things Scripture reveals as having occurred prior to Genesis 1:1. The creation of angels and the rebellion of Lucifer (Satan) are creation events that, as previously stated, I believe are part of the Genesis 1:1 *"beginning"*. God's elective choices from among all humanity were made *"before the foundation of the world"* Eph. 1:4. To accomplish the salvation of all of His "choices", the expanse of history up to this present day is required because God's will shall be done.

Isa. 46:10 Declaring the end from the beginning, and from ancient times **the things that are not yet done, saying, My counsel shall stand, and I will do all my pleasure:**

Among the other *"things that are not yet done"* is the salvation of the, as yet, unsaved, perhaps even yet unconceived, elect people. Whatever passage of time is required for the conception of, and then the salvation of His elect, will happen. Whatever time is necessary for this to occur is God's secret.

In the New Testament, Acts 4:28 echoes the truth of Isaiah 46:10, where Peter, preaching to the leadership of Israel. It says that even the actions of men must comply with God's pre- determined will.

Acts 4:27 For of a truth <u>*against thy holy child Jesus,*</u> *whom thou hast anointed, both* <u>*Herod, and Pontius*</u>

Pilate, with the Gentiles, and the people of Israel, were gathered together,

Acts 4:28 For **to do whatsoever thy hand and thy counsel determined before to be done.**

Included in the phrase *"whatsoever thy hand and thy counsel hath determined before to be done"* is the certain salvation of all of whom God has, *"...from the beginning chosen..."* All of these salvations will happen. Given the divine assurance that God will do His pleasure, Acts 15:18 must be understood in the context of Isaiah 46:10 and Acts 4:28. Remember,

Acts 15:18 **Known unto God** *are all his works from the beginning of the world.*

The denial of God's elective salvations is doctrinal stubborness to the extreme. The end of man's history cannot occur until the last elect person is at least conceived, because the fulfillment of God's work of election can be accomplished even within the womb. Therefore, regardless of whatever stage of life that "last" elect person is in, time must continue until his or her physical conception occurs because God must save "all" of His elect.

Why must all of God's elective salvations be accomplished? The truth of Romans 5:12 defines the reason.

When the "choosing verses" above are coupled to the truth of the universal fall of Rom. 5:12, it necessitates a savior.

Rom. 5:12 Wherefore, as by one man sin entered into the world, and death by sin; and so death passed upon all men, for that **all have sinned:**

Until a person is conceived, they cannot be Scripturally condemned in sin "in Adam". All of Adam's posterity are included in the Romans 5:12 verse above. The controversial, Biblical truth of election will be futher examined in Part 2 Topic 5, of this book.

From the point about the necessity of conception, some may choose to argue that this supports the indispensable role of man in the salvation miracle. Scripture defuses any such argument. David, among others, attests to the truth that God is sovereign over the events in the womb.

> *Psa. 139:13 For thou hast possessed my reins:* <u>*thou hast covered me in my mother's womb*</u>*.* *Psa. 139:14 I will praise thee; for* <u>*I am fearfully and wonderfully made*</u>*: marvellous are thy works; and that my soul knoweth right well. Psa. 139:15 My substance was not hid from thee, when* <u>*I was made in secret, and curiously wrought in the lowest parts of the earth.*</u> _ *Psa. 139:16 Thine eyes did see my substance, yet being unperfect; and* <u>*in thy book all my members were written, which in continuance were fashioned, when as yet there was none of them.*</u>

God is sovereign over all creation, all human conceptions, and all salvations.

Returning to the first example of a "gulf" placed by God, we look at the original creation account of Genesis 1, 2, and 3. No gulf or chasm existed between God and man in the time before man's fall into sin. It has always been God's purpose to dwell eternally with mankind. This purpose was stated in Revelations.

> *Rev. 21:3 And I heard a great voice out of heaven saying,* <u>*Behold, the tabernacle of God is with men,*</u>

and **he will dwell with them, and they shall be his people, and God himself shall be with them, and be their God.**

In the creation (or re-creation) account of Genesis chapters 1 and 2, death did not exist because there was, as yet, no sin in this new creation (or re-creation). Sin is the only reason for death. Therefore, eternal life and dwelling with mankind was God's plan for man, as he was created. From the Genesis account, we learn of further plans for men by God. After the seven days of the creation account, in Genesis 1:28 and 2: 15 and 16, Adam and Eve were given a list of what could be properly labeled as their life instructions and privileges in their place as creations of God.

> *Gen. 1:28 And God blessed them, and God said unto them,* **Be fruitful, and multiply**, *and* **replenish the earth, and subdue it:** *and* **have dominion** *over the fish of the sea, and over the fowl of the air, and over every living thing that moveth upon the earth*.

The list in Genesis 1:28 included: *Be fruitful, and multiply* (have children) *replenish the earth,* (meaning to "fill it" or "be full of it") (lots of descendants) *subdue it* (I will admit that I find "*subdue it*" a curious command, being placed in Genesis chapter 1, before man's fall into sin. At this point, Adam and Eve might have looked at their surroundings in the paradise of Eden and wondered what needed to be subdued. I contend that this instruction was given in God's omniscient knowledge of what lay ahead in mankind's existence on earth.), *have dominion over the fish of the sea, and over the fowl of the air, and over every living thing that moveth upon the earth.* (Rule all creation.)

Next, in Chapter 2, additional commands concerning the Garden were issued.

> *Gen. 2:15 And the LORD God took the man, and* <u>*put him into the garden of Eden to*</u> ***dress it and to*** ***keep it.*** *Gen. 2:16 And the LORD God commanded the man, saying,* ***Of every tree of the garden thou*** ***mayest freely eat:***

In the garden, they were to: "*dress it and to keep it*". God also told them where the pantry was: " *Of every tree of the garden thou mayest freely eat:*". It merits notice that there were no consequences attached for any failure to comply with the instructions in Genesis 1:28 or 2:15 & 16. However, in Genesis 2:17, God gave Adam and Eve what I submit was their gospel.

> *Gen. 2:17* ***But of the tree of the knowledge of good*** ***and evil, thou shalt not eat of it: for in the day that*** ***thou eatest thereof thou shalt surely die.***

The purpose of this command was to reveal God's authority over men and to tell them how to avoid sin (death). At this point, only God knew what the concept of death meant. His first gospel (Gen. 2:17) was given to protect man from death. All subsequent gospels will be given to provide redemption from, or out of death.

All creation, including Adam, Eve, and all mankind, were created to glorify God. Mankind was the crown jewel of God's creation because of man's unique place of being both, able to receive love from God, and obligated to give back glory, honor and power to God. This is the pleasure God purposed from His creation.

> *Rev. 4:11* <u>*Thou art worthy, O Lord, to receive glory*</u> <u>*and honour and power: for*</u> ***thou hast created all*** ***things, and for thy pleasure they are and were*** ***created.***

The proper and full expression of love by Adam and Eve could only occur by their obedience to the gospel God gave them. Obedience to Genesis 2:17 would secure their possession of eternal life and thereby avoid the penalty of eternal death. The essential characteristic of true love is that it can only be given willfully, as opposed to being produced from any form of compulsion. This is the point in time when Adam, Eve, and all men "in Adam", possessed a "true" free will. They had no predisposition to obey or disobey. By their use of their "unbiased free will" their choice between obedience and disobedience was made. This concept of man's original "free will" will be examined in depth in Part 2.

This is why I call Genesis 2:17 Adam and Eve's gospel. They were commanded to obey it and live eternally with God. Verse 17 is the first verse where disobedience is an implied voluntary option for Adam and Eve. It is the one command they received that carried a consequence for disobedience. There is no recorded question coming from Adam and Eve after they received this command. Since death was presented as an undesirable consequence, it can be reasonably concluded that they had some conception of what the word "death" meant. We also know from Gen. 3:8 that one of the privileges Adam and Eve enjoyed was being in the presence of the Lord God in the garden. After they disobeyed the gospel that God had given to them, their sin immediately caused them to hide from this privilege. They instinctively knew they had sinned. God was looking for them.

> *Gen. 3:8 And they heard the voice of the LORD God <u>walking in the garden</u> in the cool of the day: and* **<u>Adam and his wife hid themselves from the presence of the LORD God</u>** *<u>amongst the trees of the garden.</u>* *Gen. 3:9 And the* **<u>LORD God called unto Adam, and said unto him, Where art thou?</u>**

From God's question in verse 9, we see an example of where men might be tempted to see God as being limited like a man. Did God not know where Adam and Eve were and what they had done? Of course not. The scene is just presented in a conversational context between God and Adam and Eve because they existed in time and He related to them in time. At this confrontation, God exposed their sin. Because Adam and Eve, as the federal representatives of all humanity, had sinned, the first "gulf" of separation was established. God put a "fixed" barrier between Adam and Eve, (including all of mankind), and the tree of life.

> *Gen. 3:22 And the LORD God said, Behold, the man is become as one of us, to know good and evil: and now, **lest he put forth his hand, and take also of the tree of life, and eat, and live for ever:** Gen. 3:23 Therefore **the LORD God sent him forth from the garden of Eden**, to till the ground from whence he was taken. Gen. 3:24 So **he drove out the man**; and **he placed at the east of the garden of Eden Cherubims, and a flaming sword which turned every way, to keep the way of the tree of life.***

From this conversation among the Godhead, the consensus was that man and woman could not be allowed to gain eternal life by their own willful actions. At this point in Scripture, it is worthwhile to consider asking the question, "Why not?" The reason is that the sovereignty of God would have been breached, if Adam and Eve had been allowed to take this action. If they had obtained eternal life by their act of eating from the tree of life, then the grace of God could not be sovereignly credited for their salvation. They would have become sinners who had achieved their own salvation. They would have been sinners who were able to disregard the gospel given to them by God, but yet could have attained salvation by their own hand. This possibility was impermissible in the eternal plan of God.

Thus, I propose that this event is the origin of, and the first earthly application of, the *"great gulf fixed"* principle. Once the locked gate, the "Eden gulf", was established, the finality of their expulsion became obvious to Adam and Eve. They did not try to search the perimeter of the Garden to see if there was any possibility of climbing the wall and thereby sneak back in. They knew that any reentry was impossible. If God had no other plans, mankind was doomed to eternal separation from the presence of the Lord God.

But God had other plans and they are all known to Him (Acts 15:18). The first ray of hope given to Adam and Eve (and all mankind) was the prophecy issued in Genesis 3:15, where God mysteriously suggested a future defeat of their deceiver, the serpent (Satan).

> *Gen. 3:15* ___And I will put enmity between thee and the woman, and between thy seed and her seed; it shall bruise thy head, and thou shalt bruise his heel.___

Mankind would have to wait for the details of and accomplishment of this prophecy.

CHAPTER 4

The "fixed gulf" of Noah

EVICTED FROM THE PARADISE environment of Eden, man now faced a cursed creation and was left to live, not only by the sweat of his brow but also by the use of his conscience and the knowledge of good and evil that he acquired by his disobedience in the Garden. However, even prior to the eviction from the Garden, God had purposed to preserve a remnant of men by faith, which as will be proven later, is a gift of God's grace.

Nevertheless, the fallen nature of men now separated them from perfect fellowship with God, and their nature spiraled downward into the depths of evil. Because of this fallen nature, man's conscience was now, a flawed source of moral guidance. Proverbs summed up the problem of a will that makes choices under the influence of a fallen nature; a will devoid of any guidance or influence of the Holy Spirit. The problem was not that man was incapable of choosing and doing "good". Man's new natural preference in his choices was now focused on self, not on pleasing God. These choices led to death. After the expulsion from the Garden, even if a man could successfully avoid any further sinful choices, the first sin in the Garden (*of all men Rom. 5:12*) still required a payment. It was a payment which no man could make. Below is the verse that captures the natural inclination of mankind's conscience

> *Prov. 14:12 <u>There is **a way which seemeth right unto a man**</u>, but the end thereof are the ways of death.*

If continued "free will" in all of Adam's descendants was a given fact, and thus the choices of good and evil remained as equal options for man's will, it would be strange for Scripture to pointedly assert that the choice that man prefers to make is the way that leads to death? It should elicit the question of "Why does the way leading to death seem right to man?"

By Chapter 6 of Genesis, we read of God's assessment of the progress that men had achieved from their living by the dictates of a conscience under the influence of the prophesised knowledge of good and evil (Gen.3:5). Their evil ways had become an obsession. Scripture testifies to the degree of their preference for the "way leading to death".

> *Gen. 6:5 And GOD saw that **the wickedness of man was great in the earth, and that every imagination of the thoughts of his heart was only evil continually.**_*

As previously quoted, the next two verses in Chapter 6 are further examples that can easily persuade readers to view God as strictly a reactor as the narrative of man's descent into evil continues.

> *Gen. 6:6 And **it repented the LORD** that he had made man on the earth, and **it grieved him** at his heart. Gen. 6:7 And the LORD said, I will destroy man whom I have created from the face of the earth; both man, and beast, and the creeping thing, and the fowls of the air; for **it repenteth me that I have made them.**

This passage gives the impression that God is, in some way, at the mercy of the actions of mankind. For those of us who possess the completed Word of God, while such verses that seem to humanize God, it should not override our memory of Acts 15:18. Despite the emotions attributed to Him, we must remember His sovereign knowledge of all His works, including His decisions affecting all mankind.

In the book of Ezekiel, Chapter 33, the Lord God states that the death of the "wicked" does not please him. He even implores Israel not to die for their evil ways. The record of this pronouncement is in the context of a father pleading with his child to not disobey him. Although as a sovereign God, He could make Israel do His will, He communicated with them as though He was helpless to do anything but plead with them. Nevertheless, what the next verse reveals is God's emotions about sin and death.

> *Ezek. 33:11 Say unto them, As I live, saith the Lord GOD, **I have no pleasure in the death of the wicked**; but that the wicked **turn from his way and live: turn ye, turn ye from your evil ways; for why will ye die, O house of Israel?**

This verse tells us that the Lord is grieved by sin and that He desires men to turn from it. Although God can never be happy at the sin of man, sin also never occurs outside God's sovereign knowledge or control. God not only knows whom He will save from their sins, but He also knows how He will do it. He has sovereignly allowed man's fall into the bondage of sin, while also, sovereignly, He has foreordained certain people to salvation from before the beginning of time. (Eph. 1:4)

It behooves the reader to stop and consider the two distinct passages that describe God's feeling about sin (Gen. 6:6-7; Ezek. 33:11), in contrast with the two verses cited that reveal God's foreordained work of election. God's work of election of some to salvation, necessitates His plan to defeat the penalty of sin for all of His elect. (Eph. 1:4-5; 2 Thess. 2:13) It foolish to ignore the pre-creation works of God in the Ephesians and 2 Thessalonians passages just because they strain human logic. Because they seem to negate the role of the will of man and his responsibility for the actions of his will, much of Christendom does just that. Many Christians strive to bend the meaning of these verses away from any possibility that God predestined some men to salvation. Man's logic must not be allowed to construe God's will and work as being subordinate to, or dependent upon, any act of man's will.

Back to the scene described in Genesis 6:6-7, it is wrong for any Bible student to view this passage as God shifting to "plan B" just because His "plan A" seems to have failed. These verses are simply showing us that our sovereign God has emotions. It may seem logically incomprehensible that the God (Jesus Christ), who created us, and who has allowed sin to occur, can be emotionally affected by its occurrence in man. But, how can the God, whose essence is love, not have emotions about man's sin? Nevertheless, over and above all of God's emotional involvement with mankind, the truth remains that God's will is done in all things because God knows all of His plans in between the beginning and the end. God may show His emotions to events as they happen, but the emotion of surprise is never one of His emotions.

> *Dan. 4:35 And all the inhabitants of the earth are reputed as nothing: and* **he doeth according to his will in the army of heaven, and among the inhabitants of the earth**: *and none can stay his hand, or say unto him, What doest thou?*

Continuing with the Bible narrative, in response to the level of evil, that the hearts of man had sunken to, God decrees the destruction of humanity by flooding the earth. God stopped short of the total annihilation of all men by giving grace to Noah and his family.

> *Gen. 6:8 But* **Noah found grace** *in the eyes of the LORD.*

In this verse, there are two things worth noting about the word "grace". First, this verse is the first mention of the word "grace" in Scripture. Second, note that God's grace is the first personal attribute mentioned concerning Noah. It was not his faith. It was not his personal, good moral character or Noah's good works that caused *"grace to be found in the eyes of the Lord"*. If the grace found in Noah was due to anything in Noah, then God would have been showing *"respect of a man"*. Scripture denies this possibility.

> *Rom. 2:11 For* **there is no respect of persons with God**.

The grace Noah received was displayed in the form of his faithful obedience. The grace *"found"* in Noah, and the faith he displayed are the gifts of God. It would be a theological oxymoron to assert that the grace *"found"* in Noah was a self-generated quality of Noah. Grace cannot be a quality that earns God's favor. It can only be received from God. Regarding Noah's faith, it too must be a gift, as later revealed in Eph. 2:8-9, where Paul discloses, that the truth that saving faith itself is also a gift. Even though Noah's faith is cited in the faith chapter of Hebrews 11, the point is that in Genesis 6:8, we are told that Noah *"found grace in the eyes of the Lord"*, rather than God finding merit in Noah's faith.

> *Heb. 11:7* **<u>By faith Noah</u>**, *being warned of God of things not seen as yet, moved with fear, prepared an ark to the saving of his house; by the which he condemned the world, and became heir of the righteousness which is by faith.*

It was by God's grace that Noah demonstrated the gift of faith by being obedient to God's warning about the coming flood, to His commands to build the ark, and load it, as directed, with animals. It confounds the logic of man to hear that the very faith by which God saves anyone comes from the very gift of faith that God sovereignly ordained to give a person.

> *Gen. 7:5 And Noah did according unto all that the LORD commanded him.*

It also bears notice that during the estimated 55 to 75 year time period it took Noah to construct the ark, there was no record of any men who, by a presumed free will, desired, or asked, to join Noah in his project or to receive a place on the ark. Upon the ark's completion and the loading of it with the animals and Noah's family, God personally completed the work by shutting the door (Gen. 7:16).

> *Gen. 7:16 And they that went in, went in male and female of all flesh, as God had commanded him: and* **<u>the LORD shut him in.</u>**

In addition to shutting the door, the door needed to be water-proofed (sealed) with pitch like the remainder of the exterior.

> *Gen. 6:14 Make thee an ark of gopher wood; rooms shalt thou make in the ark, and* **shalt pitch it within and without with pitch.**

Physics and logic allow a presumption that the door was at the base of the ark. Genesis 6:16 tells us where the door was to be.

> *Gen. 6:16 A window shalt thou make to the ark, and in a cubit shalt thou finish it above; and* **the door of the ark shalt thou set in the side thereof;** *with lower, second, and third stories shalt thou make it.*

The ark was constructed on dry land. It had to be in a dry-dock setting. It was a tall vessel – 30 cubits in height according to Genesis 6:15. Scholars generally maintain that a cubit equated to 18 inches. If so, the height of the ark was approximately 45 feet. With the door in the side of the ark, the closing of, and water-proofing of, the door would have to be done by someone on the outside who would then "miss the boat". Granted, Noah or one of his sons could have done the exterior sealing work and then be hoisted up to the top by ropes. But any dispute about how the door was closed and sealed is answered in Genesis 7, where God makes the specific point of telling us that He shut the door.

> *Gen. 7:16 And they that went in, went in male and female of all flesh, as God had commanded him: and* **the LORD shut him in**.

When this happened, the fate of all who spurned the opportunity to believe what God told Noah, and thereby join Noah and his family, was sealed shut also. Any presumed "free will" never led anyone else to seek a place on the ark, and God made sure that there were no changes made once the door was shut. It was another visual separation set by God upon unbelieving men. It became another "gulf" that was an obvious act of God. We aren't told whether there were any who may have realized their plight and, as a result, were banging on the door to get in once the flooding began. If the flood was cataclysmic and tsunami-like in nature, as some Bible scholars suggest, there would have been no opportunity for desperate repentance by those left behind. The prophesied rapture of the body of Christ will be of the same instantaneous nature. It too will deny unbelievers any chance for a last, split-second repentance.

I suggest that the fact that God shut the door means that it sealed this judgment upon the sins of men. It was most certainly a "fixed gulf" that could not be crossed by the unchosen remainder of mankind who were shut out of the ark; for all of those who did not find, *"grace in the eyes of the Lord"*. The judgment was carried out, and the effects of it were just as God had prophesied. Noah and his family were saved, while all living things on the face of the earth perished.

> *Gen. 7:23 And **every living substance was destroyed** which was upon the face of the ground, both man, and cattle, and the creeping things, and the fowl of the heaven; and they were destroyed from the earth: and **Noah only remained alive, and they that were with him in the ark**.*

There was no reprieve for anyone who "missed that boat". Those on the outside could not keep God from closing the door. They watched the ark being built, but did not seek to join Noah. They could not question or complain to God about it.

Dan 4:35".... *none can stay his hand, or say unto him, What doest thou?"*

The "closed door of the ark" was an undeniable "gulf" of separation imposed by God upon mankind.

CHAPTER 5

The "fixed gulf" of Languages

THE PERIOD OF THE replenishing of the earth with humanity after Noah and the flood is called the dispensation of human government. The earth was re-populated through Noah, his wife, and his three sons and their wives. God made two specific physical changes to the post-flood world. The fear of man now existed in all of the replenished animal life, and the killing of animals for food was now allowed in contrast to the previous vegetarian diet that sustained man before the flood.

This was accompanied by a new moral teaching about blood. While the killing of animals for food became permissible, the consumption of their blood was forbidden. This teaching led to God's emphasis on the role of blood as the source of life in all living things. God emphasized the sanctity of the blood of man who was made in His image. He also made the shedding of any man's blood by another man a sin, punishable by the death of the killer. The responsibility to administer this punishment was now placed in the hands of men.

Gen. 9:4 ___But flesh with the life thereof, which is___
___the blood thereof, shall ye not eat.___

Gen. 9:5 *And surely your blood of your lives will I*
require; at the hand of every beast will I require it,
and at the hand of man; at the hand of every man's
brother will I require the life of man.
Gen. 9:6 ___Whoso sheddeth man's blood, by man___
___shall his blood be shed: for in the image of God___
___made he man.___

This command became the first law given to men that they were required to enforce upon other men. It introduced the concept of men governing themselves. The law of capital punishment is the most severe responsibility of a government. It is preeminent over all other laws imposed for the general purpose of maintaining civilized order among men. From this point in history, we can understand that the very concept of government is also a creation of God. In the letter of Romans, Paul details the purpose and importance of government, along with the reason for the need for respect for those who administer the government.

Rom 13:1 *Let every soul be subject unto the higher*
powers. For there is no power but of God: ___the pow-___
___ers that be are ordained of God.___
Rom 13:2 ___Whosoever therefore resisteth the pow-___
___er, resisteth the ordinance of God:___ *and they that*
resist shall receive to themselves damnation.
Rom 13:3 *For* *rulers are not a terror to good works,*
but to the evil. Wilt thou then not be afraid of the
power? do that which is good, and thou shalt have
praise of the same:

*Rom 13:4 For he is **the minister of God to thee for good**. But if thou do that which is evil, be afraid; for he beareth not the sword in vain: for **he is the minister of God, a revenger to execute wrath upon him that doeth evil**.*

As we read on in Genesis, God knew that men needed governance because the flood did not remove their fallen nature. As the narrative continues, we see that mankind, just as the angel Lucifer in his day, still lusted to be as God and reside where He resided. Using their gifts of intellect and ingenuity, they learned how to make brick and to build structures. Being of one language, they turned their desires toward the heavens and conspired to build a tower "*to reach heaven*" by their own efforts and exalt their own "*name*".

Gen. 11:3 And they said one to another, Go to, let us make brick, and burn them throughly. And <u>they had brick for stone, and slime had they for morter</u>.
*Gen. 11:4 And they said, Go to, <u>let us build us a city and a tower, whose top may **reach unto heaven**; and **let us make us a name**, lest we be scattered abroad upon the face of the whole earth</u>.*

The expressed fear of being scattered, which was the stimulus for their plans to build a tower to reach heaven, deserves some consideration. God had commanded man to "replenish the earth" in two prior occasions in scripture – Genesis 1:28, and immediately after the flood, in Genesis 9:1.

*Gen. 1:28 And God blessed them, and God said unto them, Be fruitful, and multiply, and **replenish the earth**,....*

> *Gen. 9:1 And God blessed Noah and his sons, and said unto them, Be fruitful, and multiply, and <u>replenish the earth.</u>*

The word "replenish" comes from the Hebrew word "male" or "mala". It means "to fill" or "to be full". It is used in connection with the earth. Thus the command of God in both cases is for man, both in the Garden and immediately after the flood, to "fill the earth". Therefore the "anti-scattering" plans of the men in Genesis 11:4 were in direct defiance of God's commands.

Please allow me another moment of digression to provide some interesting food for thought about the word "replenish". The phrase "<u>replenish the earth,...</u>" as found in Chapter 1 verse 28, conveys a curious implication. The normal meaning of "replenish" is "to fill again". Ask yourself, "When was it filled the first time? In the context of Genesis 9:1, we understand that the flood had emptied the earth of all living creatures. Therefore, it needed to be "filled again". Noah and his sons were commanded to do this.

However, in Genesis 1:28, where the same word appears, the concept of "refilling" seems out of place. If all of Genesis 1 is describing the first creation, the command of Genesis 1:28 should have been translated as, "plenish (fill) the earth." But maybe, "replenish" is a more fitting translation than it seems at first glance. My personal view is that it is plausible that the command to replenish could be contextually connected to an event that is only alluded to earlier in Genesis. Between "the beginning" of Genesis 1:1 and six-day creation activity of God, starting with Genesis 1:3, there is the curious verse 2, which as noted in Chapter 2, seems to be a contextual misfit with the rest of this Chapter.

Gen. 1:2 And the earth was without form, and void; and darkness was upon the face of the deep. And the Spirit of God moved upon the face of the waters.

If one thinks about it, the inclusion of, and wording of, Genesis 1:2 seems out of place with the tone of the rest of Chapter 1. It seems to suggest some sort of transitional period between the verse 1 "beginning" and the "day one" of verse 3. Although this is pure, but not entirely unreasonable, conjecture on my part, this "period" in verse 2 could have an obscure, but plausible explanation. If the creation that was made *"in the beginning"* had been interrupted by a destructive judgment of the Creator upon it, perhaps because of the sin and fall of Lucifer and one-third of the angels, the bleak and dark language of verse 2 is understandable. If this interpretation is valid, then the actions that commence in verse 3 might be more accurately understood as a "re-creation". If verse 3 starts the account of a "re-creation", then God's command to *"replenish the earth"* would be more contextually appropriate.

This is not an entirely unwarranted speculation. I do not offer this speculation in any attempt suggest a "gap theory" that is used in some theological circles for the sake of explaining the appearance of age in the earth, and thereby accommodating those who advocate for the existence of an "old earth". Regardless of the "age" of our planet and universe, God is entirely capable of creating any appearance of "age". I am making this theological speculation based upon the mysterious tone of verse 2 when it is contrasted with the positive language of the rest of Genesis chapter 1. The contextual tension of Genesis 1:2 with the rest of Chapter 1 deserves, at least, some theological consideration.

Returning to the prideful undertaking of the tower builders, God looked down on this and saw that it was the fact of men having only one language that was enabling them to conspire and co-operate in this prideful work.

> *Gen. 11:6 And the LORD said, Behold, __the people is__* *__one, and they have all one language;__ and this they* *begin to do: and now __nothing will be restrained__* *__from them, which they have imagined to do.__*

Once more men's imaginations led them into displeasure with God. In response, God moved to introduce the next "fixed gulf" to obstruct this sinful work of men.

> *Gen. 11:7 Go to, __let us go down, and there con-__* *__found their language, that they may not under-__* *__stand one another's speech.__*

The result of the confusing of human language by God remains is yet another stark testimony of His existence. The phenomenon of languages presents a serious challenge to evolutionary theory. In nature, I see many examples of God's creations in the animal kingdom that present serious biological challenges to evolutionists. I respectfully challenge evolutionists to explain the existence of such contradictions of nature as, the zebra, a firefly, a hummingbird or a bat, etc. Think about how the unique physical features of these random species present a serious challenge to any feasible evolutionary explanation. Likewise, the existence of the sheer volume of, and the diversity of, human languages presents a similar evolutionary dilemma that defies explanation. I believe that the multitude of diverse human languages presents an insurmountable challenge to evolutionary theory. For example, how did such vastly dissimilar languages, such as English and Chinese, come into existence from among one, supposedly, "evolved" species of creation - man?

As of 2009, the Bible alone has been translated into 2,508 languages. (source: Linguisticsociety.com) How can evolutionists, for example, explain the existence of two groups of people, whom they theorize, ascended from the same primordial slime, with the same, basic physiological make-up, evolve to possess such dissimilar languages and alphabets, such as English and Chinese, let alone any of the other 2,508 known languages? If man shared a common evolutionary history, then their method of communication should have likewise displayed a high degree of continued uniformity. Evolutionists must grant that the same primordial evolutionary processes which produced man, also produced the horse and the rabbit. I dare to suggest that, today, a horse or rabbit in China would have no problem communicating with a horse or rabbit in the United States. Their communicating language would be the same. I cannot be dogmatic about this, but I postulate that there is not another species of living creatures that display the diversity of language than that of mankind. If mankind is the product of an evolutionary process, how can this be explained?

I believe the Biblical account of God's work of creation. Language is a facet of that creation and was created by God for his communications with the prime focus of His love – man. Adam and Eve didn't have to go to language school. The gift of language was given to men to allow them to commune with God and rule the earth that He gave them dominion over. Scripture confirms that as the earth's population grew, that only one language existed as stated in Genesis 11:6 above. That verse was the fuel for the anti-scattering conspiracy that was being attempted by men, as noted in verse 4.

> *Gen. 11:4 And they said, Go to, <u>let us build us a city and a tower</u>, whose top may reach unto heaven; and let us make us a name, **lest we be scattered** <u>abroad upon the face of the whole earth.</u>*

So in Genesis 11:7, we see how, by one sovereign act, God confounds their communication abilities by the imposition of the diverse languages that He placed upon men. This supernatural work of God displays another barrier or gulf set by God to block man's attempt to attain glory by their own efforts.

The concept of the origin of language is worthy of contemplation. Can the evolutionists possibly explain how a sentence, that is spoken or read by one person would read: "God is love.", while the same sentence, is spoken or read by another person on the same planet, would read: "上帝就是 爱" ? The Bible has a perfect explanation for the phenomenon of human languages. It was a purposed work of a sovereign God. This act of God was the cause of humanity's dispersal and prevented any further similar building efforts. God was not happy with this rebellious tower building venture of men. Nevertheless, both statements, "God is love" and "上帝就是爱" , announce the same truth. Genesis 11:8 tells us what God accomplished by the confounding of languages.

Gen. 11:8 So ***the LORD scattered them abroad*** *from thence upon the face of all the earth: and* ***they left off to build the city.***

The "fixed gulf" of confounded language sovereignly accomplished the prevention of any attempt by men to reach God by their own hands. This "gulf" was yet another "obvious gulf "created by an act of a sovereign God for a specific purpose. The imposed language confusion forced men to scatter as God had commanded them.

Once scattered, however, God did not prevent this gulf from being overcome by men. God gave man the ability to learn the languages of other separated groups of men. He allowed them to inter-communicate by the ability of men to become multilingual. One reason He would allow this was that, after their "scattering", God knew that he would eventually provide a gospel that He wanted all men to hear. To further facilitate the spread of the gospel among men of diverse languages, God also acted to bless men, temporarily, with the supernatural sign gift of speaking in tongues of other languages to facilitate the spread of his word.

Nevertheless, the creation of the "gulf" of languages was a sudden, and God-imposed work upon men for the purpose of fulfilling the command to scatter and have dominion over the earth. There is no logic to explain how or why humanity could or would "evolve" into such diverse forms of oral and written communication. I believe that the "language gulf" was yet another sovereign, immediate act of God. It stands as another example of the truth that says, "....*none can stay his hand.*"

> *Dan. 4:35 And all the inhabitants of the earth are reputed as nothing: and he doeth according to his will in the army of heaven, and among the inhabitants of the earth: and <u>none can stay his hand, or say unto him, What doest thou?</u>*

CHAPTER 6

The "fixed gulf" of Abraham

THE NEXT THREE "FIXED gulfs" to be discussed are ones established by God that were not immediately apparent to their recipients. They heard what the Lord commanded of them and perceived no problem of compliance with the particular commands. These are the "fixed gulfs" that I label as "subtle" in nature. The first one involves Abraham. Picking up the Genesis narrative after the confounding of languages:

> *Gen. 11:9 Therefore is the name of it called Babel; because the LORD did there confound the language of all the earth: and **from thence did the LORD scatter them abroad upon the face of all the earth**.*

Mankind was scattered as God ordained it. Starting with verse 10 of Genesis Chapter 11 and running to verse 27, we find a genealogical record of Noah's oldest son, Shem. As this list unfolds, it only mentions and tracks the line through specific individuals, despite the repetitive description of each generation as having "sons and daughters". The earth was being populated. When one traces the list down to verse 27, it stops at the generation of Abraham, Nahor, and Haran, who were born to Terah. This verse also includes a curious additional mention of a son, Lot, being born to Haran. (As we know, Lot surfaces later in the narrative about Abraham's life.) Starting at verse 28, the narrative moves to the description about some particulars of Abram's life and how he ended up in Haran of the Chaldees with Terah, his father, Nahor, his brother, and Lot, his nephew. Haran, Abraham's other brother, had died before they moved.

About the year 2000 B.C., God sovereignly chose to bestow some specific blessings on this pagan man named Abram, who was living in Ur of the Chaldees, located in what is today, Iraq. (consider the irony). Genesis 12 opens with God speaking with him. It is interesting that, as this chapter opens, there are no reasons offered for God's selection of Abram to receive the blessings and instructions that He will proceed to give him. Before revealing the "fixed gulf" created by God's choosing of Abram, the actual selection of Abram by God, needs to be reviewed. First, in Genesis 12, the narrative of Scripture focuses in on this pagan man, Abram.

> *Gen. 12:1 Now the **LORD had said unto Abram, Get thee out of thy country**, and from thy kindred, and from thy father's house, **unto a land that I will shew thee***

John Gill (1797 – 1871), an English Baptist preacher, Bible scholar, and theologian wrote the following in his Bible commentary about the significance of God's command to this man to "*Get thee out of thy country*". Gill wrote:

> *"**get thee out of thy country**; the land of Chaldea, and the city of Ur, which was in it, or out of Meso-*

potamia, in which, when taken in a large sense, were both Ur and Haran; and this country was now become idolatrous, for though it was first inhabited and peopled by the posterity of Shem in the time of Arphaxad, yet these, in process of time, degenerated from the true religion, and fell into idolatry. The same Maimonides (w) calls Zabaeans, in whose faith and religion, he says, Abram was brought up, and who asserted there was no other God but the sun, moon, and stars; and these Zabaeans, as he relates from their books and annals, say of Abram themselves, that he was educated in Cuthia, and dissented from the common people; and asserted, that besides the sun, there was another Creator; to whom they objected, and so disputes arose among them on this subject: now Abram being convinced of idolatry, is called out from those people, and to have no fellowship with them; it is literally in the Hebrew text (x), "go to thee out of thy country"; for thy profit and good, as Jarchi interprets it; as it must be to quit all society with such an idolatrous and superstitious people."

John Gill's Exposition of the Entire Bible

Given this historical background about Abram and where he lived, this act of God's choosing of Abram should inspire some questions. Two key questions need to be addressed, "Why did God choose Abram?" and "Why did Abram obey with no questions asked?" I do not find any substantiation for Gill's claim that Abram was "convinced of the idolatry", but nonetheless, Abram complied without an argument. These questions take us directly to the subjects of God's prerogative of electing (choosing) of men to salvation and of what happens within those whom He chooses. (These topics will be addressed in depth later.) Here are some other questions worth asking: Did Abram's response in faith to God's instructions equate to his salvation? Yes, because Scripture later tells us that salvation comes by faith alone (Rom. 10:17) and that Abram's faith response brought imputed righteousness to him (Rom. 4:3). Righteousness only comes to believers. Did Abram know why God chose him? No. Without reasoning, questioning or bargaining on his part, what caused Abram's obedience? Something caused God to speak to this particular pagan man, and something happened within Abram to precipitate his obedience. God's speaking to Abram in Genesis 12:1 may seem like an arbitrary act of God, but God does not do "arbitrary". Remember:

> *"Known to God from the beginning are all his works." Acts 15:18*

and

> *".......he doeth according to his will in the army of heaven, and among the inhabitants of the earth: ...."* Dan. 4:35

plus

> *".......him* (God) *who worketh all things after the counsel of his own will:" Eph. 1:11*

The silence of Genesis 12 about any facts of God's elective choice, does not refute its occurrence. Today, we enjoy the benefit of the completed Word of God. A real fact of the blessing of having the completed revelation of God's Word is that we can understand that God must have produced Abram's salvation by the same foreordained choice that God applies to every salvation

(Eph. 1:4). They are all ordained (chosen) by His will from before the foundation of the world. This is the only answer to the "Why?" questions about salvation; Abraham's or that of anyone else.

For Christians today, the components of the salvation process have been completely revealed in Scripture. There are four specific, sovereignly performed works of God that precede every salvation. These works are listed in Part 2, Topic 8 of this book. I also provide a complete discussion of them in my previous book, "99% Grace?". If one delves into the New Testament and seeks answers to such crucial questions as: "Why does God save some and not others?"; "How does he save anyone?"; "What is the state of man's will after the fall?"; "What role does man's will play in his salvation?"; "Where does saving faith come from?"; etc.; the Biblical answers to all of these questions will emerge. To all who seek it, God's Word will reveal the connected, essential and non-contradictory truth about how saving faith occurs.

There is a vital Biblical context in which these questions are answered. This context is the revealed Scriptural truth that, regarding the Scriptural fundamentals, salvation is a uniformly accomplished act of God. If God does not impartially save all persons by the same process and for the same reason, then it must be asked, "Why not?" The only satisfactory "because" answer to this question comes from these combined biblical facts: the gift of salvation must be "granted", (Phil. 1:29), to all who "are ordained", (Acts 13:48), to receive it because they were, chosen from before the foundation of the world", (Eph. 1:4).

If there is no uniformity to the mechanics of how God saves men, and of the reason why He saves them, then it means that God must show differing respect (regard) for some people apart from others. However, the New Testament, repeatedly affirms that God is "no respecter of persons". Peter and Paul repeatedly confirmed this truth.

*Act 10:34 Then Peter opened his mouth, and said, Of a truth I perceive that **God is no respecter of persons:***

*Rom 2:11 For **there is no respect of persons with God**.*

*Eph. 6:9 And, ye masters, do the same things unto them, forbearing threatening: knowing that your Master also is in heaven; **neither is there respect of persons with him**.*

*Col. 3:25 But he that doeth wrong shall receive for the wrong which he hath done: and **there is no respect of persons**.*

*1 Pet. 1:17 And if ye call on **the Father, who without respect of persons judgeth** according to every man's work, pass the time of your sojourning here in fear:*

The phrase, *"no respect of persons"*, is a profound truth in the question about the origin of saving faith. Why? If God bestowed salvation because an individual self-generated their faith, then it means that God was saving them "in respect" of whatever was the cause of their self-generated faith. The *"no respecter of persons"* will be a repeated point of emphasis in this study.

Scripture, in Ephesians 2:8-9, teaches that the faith which brings salvation is "**the** gift of God".

Eph 2:8 For ye are saved by grace, through faith; and this not of yourselves; it is the gift of God:

Eph 2:9 Not of works, lest any man should boast.

If it is true for any believer, that the "gift of faith", which is, *"not of oneself"* - *"lest any man should boast"*, then it must be true for all who believe. God would be a "respecter of persons" to give this gift to some and not others, based upon their achievement of individual faith. Ephesians 2:8-9 makes a specific point about a singular gift. Of the three subjects mentioned at the beginning of verse 8: grace, salvation (saved) and faith, only one of these can be the focus of the singular "gift" point that Paul is making. It would be superfluous (a tautology) for Paul to tell his audience that either grace, or salvation, is "the gift" because there is no logical reason to tell people that grace and salvation are *"not of themselves"*. It would be totally illogical for anyone to boast about (take credit for) "grace" or their "salvation".

But the revelation that the faith (that saves) is "the gift" under discussion in Ephesians 2:8 is a new disclosure. The first personal sensation of saving faith (belief) seems like a self-produced experience to most people. It feels like a new mental conclusion that they have reached. However, at this moment of belief, all new believers are unaware of the inner workings of the Holy Spirit, as well as the predestined choice of God, that brought them to their step of faith. The truth of the workings of God that must precede all salvations is still is a revelation that many Christians never acknowledge. Regardless of how one interprets Ephesians 2:8-9, faith cannot be ignored as being "a gift". It is a clear doctrinal truth that gifts cannot be earned. (See Part 2, Topic 2 that clarifies the distinction between "gifted faith" and "free will faith", which must be a work.)

The root cause for God's choice of Abram was not a show of any "respect" of him, but rather it was because of the truth of God's foreordained choice of Abram; a truth that we don't learn of in Scripture until Ephesians, Chapter 1. Abram was chosen in Genesis 12:1 because he had been chosen by God before the beginning of the world, as Paul revealed in Ephesians 1:4. The controversial topic of God's predestinating choice of men is the focus of Part 2, Topic 5. There, the supposed contradiction of God having *"no respect of persons"* and His foreordination of a specific portion of mankind to salvation, is addressed. Both of the principles mentioned above of "no respect" and "foreordained faith" apply to God's choosing of Abram. It is the reason why I assert that Abraham's saving faith, as praised in the faith chapter, Hebrews 11, was the result of a sovereignly ordained choice and a sovereignly given "gift of faith". Review these facts.

1. Abram was a non-descript, idolatrous pagan with no virtue worthy of God speaking to him.
2. It was neither Terah nor Lot, to whom God spoke in Genesis 12:1.
3. Abram did not know who this God was that spoke to him.
4. Abram was not sitting around, waiting to hear from God.

Returning to the subject of Abraham's "fixed gulf", it was the result of an aspect of the promises that God made to him in Genesis 12: 2 and 3. The genealogy of Genesis 11 sets up a theologically seismic shift of focus by God away from all humanity to one man - Abram. Genesis chapter 12 marks the start of this seismic shift.

> *Gen. 12:1* **_Now the LORD had said unto Abram_**, *Get thee out of thy country, and from thy kindred, and from thy father's house, unto a land that I will shew thee:*
> *Gen. 12:2 And* **_I will make of thee a great nation_**, *and I will bless thee, and make thy name great; and thou shalt be a blessing:*
> *Gen. 12:3 And* **_I will bless them that bless thee, and curse him that curseth thee:_** *and* **_in thee shall all families of the earth be blessed._**
> *Gen. 12:4* **_So Abram departed, as the LORD had spoken unto him;_** *and Lot went with him: and Abram was seventy and five years old when he departed out of Haran.*

In verse 2 Abram is told that God, *"...will make of thee a great nation"*. The word *"nation"* is singular. In verse 3, God tells Abram that *"....in thee shall all families of the earth be blessed."* Abraham could not have perceived any "gulf" by these promises. The only natural conclusion that Abram could draw from these promises was that he needed to produce a male heir for a *"great nation"* to occur. In other words, Abraham would have thought, "Okay, I can do this." Fulfillment of this promise would depend upon Abraham's willing participation to produce some offspring. But unknown to Abraham, God would put a personal "fixed gulf" upon Sarah by closing her womb to childbearing. It was a "subtle gulf" imposed by God, but it was insurmountable to Abraham. This blocked promise served to display God's sovereign independence from any degree of reliance upon man's co-operation in the ultimate accomplishment of His will. It also served as a test of the return of Abraham's faith in trusting God to keep His promises even when they seemed hopeless and unreachable.

At first, Abraham tried to cross this particular "fixed gulf" by his fleshly attempt to supply an heir through Hagar, Sarah's handmaid. Notice that it was through Sarah, who was also aware of the *"nation"* promise, that the plan of involving Hagar was devised. Abraham, similar to Adam, submitted to his wife's idea. But God displayed His power by giving Abraham and Sarah a son only after they were both well past natural childbearing ages. This minor, but very real"gulf", though unperceived at first to Abraham, served God's purpose. God sovereignly enabled Abraham and Sarah to cross this specific "gulf" which He put on them. God, thereby, fulfilled His promises, apart from any dependence upon man (Abraham in this case).

Notice again, in Genesis 12:2, God says *"I will."*, not *"you and I will"*, or *"If you will....then I will...."*. In His relationship with Israel, God certainly made conditional promises to them that were contingent upon their willful obedience. But, when the use of a qualifier *"if"* is absent, then God's promises are unilateral.

He puts no dependence upon any willful act of man. Such promises and prophecies of God certainly involve man's actions, but God must bring them about. For example, God made prophesies about Nebuchadnezzar's conquering of, and Cyrus's releasing of, the nation of Israel hundreds of years before their fulfillment. Such promises and prophecies of God are displays of His sovereignty.

So God demonstrated that the fulfillment of His promise to Abraham would occur through him, however, it was not dependent upon the free will of, or the work of Abraham. This "subtle, yet fixed gulf", and it's God-supplied remedy, served to fortify Abraham's faith when later on, he showed his total willingness to obey God's command to him to sacrifice the very son of promise, Isaac, who had been miraculously provided to him. By faith, Abraham now knew that God would, somehow, be able to keep His initial promises made to him. The purpose of God's "gulf" in Abraham's life was accomplished.

CHAPTER 7

The "fixed gulf" of Israel

So the unilateral covenant God made with Abraham was passed, as promised, down through his descendants in the line of Isaac, then Jacob. It resulted in the formation of God's chosen nation of people – Israel. The twelve sons of the patriarch Jacob, who is also called Israel (Gen, 32:28), became the fathers of the twelve tribes of Israel. After 400 years of captivity in Egypt, Moses is chosen by God to lead Israel out of their captivity and into the promised land of Canaan.

This period of Bible history is commonly referred to as the dispensation of promise. The distinctive event of this new dispensation is God's promise of a chosen people that will come from among Abraham's descendants, with whom God will have a personal spiritual relationship. With this choice of a specific group of people, a new, "fixed gulf" was created that had duel implications. The dual aspects of the new "fixed gulf" are applied separately; one to God's chosen people group, Israel, and the other to the Gentiles. Both of these new, two-pronged "fixed gulfs" were initially, generally imperceptible to both Israel and the Gentiles.

One implication of this new, but subtle "gulf" for every Gentile (non-Israelite) was the fact that by God's new covenant with Israel, there was now no direct contact or access to God available to the Gentiles. The only salvation hope that a Gentile had was to become a proselyte of Israel. Furthermore, God's general instructions to Israel regarding Gentiles was for them to maintain a separation from the Gentiles and their false gods. God ordained that the process of any Gentile salvation could only be exclusively accomplished through a conversion to Judaism. Interestingly, God did not command any missionary effort by Israel to reach the Gentiles. In the Old Testament, 117 verses use the word "stranger" as an interchangeable word used to describe a Gentile. Most of these usages of the word "stranger" are spoken towards Israel regarding their conduct and contact with anyone who was not of Israel. Mandatory separation from "strangers" was the theme of many of these verses.

In the New Testament gospels, Jesus explicitly, during His earthly ministry, told his disciples whom He sent out to preach the gospel of the kingdom, to avoid the Gentiles.

> *Mat. 10:5 These twelve Jesus sent forth, and com-*
> *manded them, saying,* ***Go not into the way of the***
> ***Gentiles, and into any city of the Samaritans en-***
> ***ter ye not:***

Even after Christ had ascended to heaven, the evangelism restriction remained in practice, despite the commission of the Lord recorded in Matthew 28.

> *Acts 11:19 Now they which were scattered abroad*
> *upon the persecution that arose about Stephen trav-*

elled as far as Phenice, and Cyprus, and Antioch,
preaching the word to none but unto the Jews only.

In the post-resurrection missionary commissions of Jesus Christ to the disciples, their efforts were directed to Judea first and finished with the *"uttermost part of the earth"* (Acts 1:8). Only in the Millenium reign of Christ, when the kingdom of heaven on earth is established, will Israel evangelize the nations of the world.

So by the formation of the nation of Israel, all of non-Israelite humanity (Gentiles) was now separated from any relationship with God by a subtle, but real, "fixed gulf". It was not perceived as a problem by the Gentiles, because they had no natural desire to be reconciled to God. Any desire to come to God at that time of history, just as is true today, can only be genuinely implant-ed by God. Man can only "come to God" by His ordained will and means. The reconciliation restriction for all men, Jew and Gentile, would be later re-defined by Jesus speaking in John 6 and 14, where two contexts of "coming" to God are defined. The terms of these "comings" are presented in Part 2, Topic 9.

The second implication of the "fixed gulf" regarding God's choice of, and formation of, the nation of Israel as His people, is revealed by the course of Israel's history. It followed a cir-cuitous path that put them into the other part of the "dual, yet subtle fixed gulf" predicament, which they did not perceive. God had personally led them through His interaction with Moses in the 40-year exodus journey to the land that God had promised through Abraham. It was during this time that God handed down the Law to Israel, through Moses, to direct their spiritual, per-sonal and civil life as a nation. The moral part of the Law, with the Ten Commandments as the foundation, became a "subtle, fixed gulf" to Israel. They did not perceive any problems with these commandments. This unawareness happened because, on a point by point basis, there were no demands of the Law that any individual Jew viewed as impossible to keep. Even when the level of required total obedience to the Law was openly and repeatedly taught to them, Israel repeatedly promised to obey. It was a promise that they repeatedly broke because it was a promise that they, by their self-wills, could never perfectly keep. Their obedience short-coming was a problem that was unperceived by Israel until after the ascension of Christ. God's law-keeping standards were clear. Israel can never plead ignorance about what God demanded of them. Read these verses and observe the underlined sections and the bold print word "**all**":

> *Exo. 23:22 But* ___if thou shalt indeed obey his voice,___ ___and do___ **all** ___that I speak;___ **then** *I will be an enemy unto thine enemies, and an adversary unto thine adversaries.*
>
> *Lev. 20:22 Ye shall therefore* ___keep___ **all** ___my statutes,___ ___and___ **all** ___my judgments,___ *and do them: that the land, whither I bring you to dwell therein, spue you not out.*
>
> *Deu. 5:29 O that there were such an heart in them, that they would fear me, and* ___keep___ **all** ___my commandments always,___ *that it might be well with them, and with their children for ever!*
>
> *Deu. 6:2 That thou mightest fear the LORD thy God,* ___to keep___ **all** ___his statutes and his commandments,___ *which I command thee, thou, and thy son, and thy son's son, all the days of thy life; and that thy days may be prolonged.*
>
> *Deu. 11:8 Therefore shall ye* ___keep___ **all** ___the commandments___ *which I command you this day, that ye may be strong, and go in and possess the land, whither ye go to possess it;*
>
> *Deu. 11:22 For if ye shall* ___diligently keep___ **all** ___these___ ___commandments___ *which I command you, to do them,*

to love the LORD your God, to walk in all his ways, and to cleave unto him; which I command thee this day, to do that which is right in the eyes of the LORD thy God.

*Deu. 17:19 And it shall be with him, and he shall read therein all the days of his life: that he may learn to fear the LORD his God, to keep **all** the words of this law and these statutes, to do them:*

*Deu. 19:9 If thou shalt <u>keep **all** these command-ments to do them</u>, which I command thee this day, to love the LORD thy God, and to walk ever in his ways; then shalt thou add three cities more for thee, beside these three:*

*Deu. 27:1 And Moses with the elders of Israel com-manded the people, saying, <u>Keep **all** the command-ments which I command you this day.</u>*

*Deu. 30:2 And shalt return unto the LORD thy God, and <u>shalt obey his voice according to **all** that I com-mand thee this day</u>, thou and thy children, with all thine heart, and with all thy soul;*

*Deu. 30:8 And thou shalt return and <u>obey the voice of the LORD, and do **all** his commandments</u> which I command thee this day.*

*2 Kings 17:13 Yet the LORD testified against Israel, and against Judah, by all the prophets, and by all the seers, saying, Turn ye from your evil ways, and keep my commandments and my statutes, <u>according to **all** the law which I commanded your fathers</u>, and which I sent to you by my servants the prophets.*

*Jer. 7:23 But this thing commanded I them, saying, <u>Obey my voice</u>, and I will be your God, and ye shall be my people: and <u>walk ye in **all** the ways that I have commanded you</u>, that it may be well unto you.*

Jer. 11:4 Which I commanded your fathers in the day that I brought them forth out of the land of Egypt, from the iron furnace, saying, <u>Obey my voice, and do them, according to all which I command you</u>: so shall ye be my people, and I will be your God:

There should not be any question about the meaning of the word *"all"*. There may be other similar verses, but the list above eliminates, as an excuse, any ignorance of the perfect law-keeping standard required of Israel. Does the word *"all"* in all of the above verses truly mean all? After Christ's ascension, the leader of the church of Jewish believers, James, understood the meaning of *"all"*. He knew the requirement was still in effect and preached accordingly.

Jas. 2:10 For whosoever shall keep the whole law, and yet <u>offend in one point, he is guilty of all</u>.

The word "all" is like a hammer that pounded the point upon them. But this hammered point would reveal a real, yet "subtle fixed gulf" for Israel. They saw nothing in the Law that was beyond their ability to obey. But if law-keeping was the standard for salvation for Israel, and *"all"* meant *"all"* in the Old Testament verses, then the repeated truth, as James wrote it, made salvation by the law unattainable. In their human pride, the little word *"all"* as not perceived as a problem. It was as if Satan continually whispered in their ears, "Oh God does not truly mean *"all"*.

A New Gospel is Introduced

After hundreds of years of law-keeping and subsequent sacrificing for failures, the true "fixed gulf" of the law went largely unrecognized, until Peter's acknowledgment of it at the Council of Jerusalem meeting with Paul. When the Pharisees pressed

Paul to require his Gentile converts to *"keep the law"*, Peter, remembering his experience at the house of Cornelius, concluded that God was now presenting salvation in a new context. Read the following text as Peter confesses the law to be an unbearable burden.

> *Acts 15:5 But <u>there rose up certain of the sect of the</u>*
> *<u>Pharisees which believed, saying</u>, That it was **need-**
> **ful to <u>circumcise them, and to command them to</u>**
> **<u>keep the law of Moses</u>**.*
> *Acts 15:6 And the apostles and elders came together*
> *for to consider of this matter.*
> *Acts 15:7 And when there had been much disputing,*
> ***<u>Peter rose up</u>**, and said unto them, Men and breth-*
> *ren, ye know how that a good while ago God made*
> *choice among us, that the Gentiles by my mouth*
> *should hear the word of the gospel, and believe.*
> *Acts 15:8 And God, which knoweth the hearts, bare*
> *them witness, giving them the Holy Ghost, even as*
> *he did unto us;*
> *Acts 15:9 And put no difference between us and*
> *them, purifying their hearts by faith.*
> *Acts 15:10 **<u>Now therefore why tempt ye God, to</u>***
> ***<u>put a yoke upon the neck of the disciples, which</u>***
> ***<u>neither our fathers nor we were able to bear?</u>***

What was the "yoke"? The Law of Moses. Verse 10 above provides another clear reason that there had to be two gospels under discussion at this Council. The gospel of grace is never called a "burden" or "yoke" (of bondage) in Scripture. Peter had acknowledged that the Law was a yoke ("gulf") because it could not be borne (kept) perfectly by any man to the achieving of salvation. The recital of the *"all"* verses above, regarding how much law must be obeyed, attests to God's requirement of perfection.

The "*all*" requirement created the "yoke". One reason why even the Jews in the Old Testament, who were true believers in the promises and prophecies from God, could not perfectly obey was because no one possessed the indwelling of the Holy Spirit. Peter finished with his conclusion of the difference between the gospel the twelve preached (the gospel of the kingdom) and the gospel which Paul had received and preached to the Gentiles (the gospel of grace).

The previously understood context for any Gentile salvation was that it could only be completed through their conversion to Judaism; a conversion that required circumcision and law-keeping. This fact is pronounced in Acts 15:5 above, where it was called "*needful*". But a fact many teachers of this verse fail to see is the clarification of who was speaking. The demand for circumcision and law-keeping was the position of the Pharisees "*which believed*". These were Pharisees who had come to believe that the Jesus of Nazareth, whom they crucified, was the prophesied Messiah of Israel. It was not the Pharisees of unbelieving Israel. Any unbelieving Pharisees would not have been attending this particular council, because they remained in total rejection of the belief that Jesus was the promised Messiah. Peter responds to these Pharisees, "*which believed*", by making this startling confession before the Council. It was a confession that unbelieving Pharisees would have stoned him for:

> *Acts 15:11 But we believe that through the grace of the Lord Jesus Christ **we shall be saved, even as they.***

The "we" and "they" stated in this verse was an understood distinction by Peter's audience. "We" meant the Jews while "they" refers to the Gentiles. How were "they" to be saved? – by faith alone; not through keeping the law – a new distinction. Peter makes this profound declaration by saying that future Jewish salvation will be in the same manner as that of the Gentiles. He is pointing out that a gospel change was happening. Remember, that Peter's comprehension of the situation and his startling declaration at the Council was not the result of a superior intellect. Peter was exhibiting the truth that he recorded in his second epistle. Peter's assertion in verse 11 was prophesied through him by the Holy Spirit. What was true of Old Testament prophets was true for Peter and all New Testament writers. Prophecy was not an intellectual achievement.

> *2 Pet. 1:21 For the **prophecy came not in old time by the will of man**: but holy men of God spake as they were moved by the Holy Ghost.*

Peter's conclusion about the change in the gospel message was the work and moving of the Holy Spirit within him. Paul's account of this confrontational Council meeting offers even further confirmation that he, Paul, had been given a different gospel by Jesus Christ than what the twelve had been given.

> *Gal. 2:2 And I went up by revelation, and **communicated unto them that gospel which I preach among the Gentiles**, but privately to them which were of reputation, lest by any means I should run, or had run, in vain.*

If there had been no difference in Paul's gospel, then no "communicating" (explaining) of his gospel would have been needed. He would have just confirmed that he preached the same message as they did. But after Paul had "communicated" his gospel to them, verses 7-9 describe the acknowledgment of the difference by both sides. It resulted in the conclusion of the Council's leadership that Paul records in verses 7-9.

*Gal. 2:7 But contrariwise, **when they saw that the gospel of the uncircumcision was committed unto me, as the gospel of the circumcision** was unto Peter;*

Gal. 2:8 (For he that wrought effectually in Peter to the apostleship of the circumcision, the same was mighty in me toward the Gentiles:)

*Gal. 2:9 And **when James, Cephas, and John, who seemed to be pillars, perceived** the grace that was given unto me, **they gave to me and Barnabas the right hands of fellowship; that we should go unto the heathen, and they unto the circumcision.***

The conclusion of both Peter and Paul at the crucial Council of Jerusalem meeting was the revelation of two different gospels.

"the gospel of the uncircumcision" and "the gospel of the circumcision".

The Savior in both gospels is the same, but the details of belief in each gospel differ.

Israel would later learn that salvation by the works of obedience to the Law was a dead end path because, as Paul writes in Roman 11, there was a new context of salvation for the "remnant" of Israel.

*Rom. 11:5 Even so then at this present time also there is **a remnant according to the election of grace.***

*Rom 11:6 And **if by grace, then is it no more of works**: otherwise grace is no more grace. But if **it** be of works, then is **it** no more grace: otherwise work is no more work.*

The pronoun *"it"* used in verse 6 is referring to the *"remnant according to the election by grace"* mentioned in verse 5. Paul is teaching that the "election" of this "remnant" is by grace, not works. Thus, even perfect law-keeping leading to salvation was a theoretical impossibility according to the truth of Romans 11:6. Works cannot make anyone God's elect. Israel, under the law, was in bondage to a truly "subtle, fixed gulf" system of salvation. It was not even a problem of mental inability that blocked Israel's comprehension of the "gulf" that the law represented. God blocked their comprehension. Israel was bound, by God, into spiritual blindness and deafness to this "subtle gulf". Jesus alludes to this "gulf" in Matthew 13 when He explains His practice of teaching by the use of parables.

> *Mat. 13:13 Therefore* <u>speak I to them</u> (Israel) <u>in parables: because they seeing see not; and hearing they hear not, neither do they understand.</u>
> *Mat. 13:14 And* <u>in them is fulfilled the prophecy of Esaias</u>, *which saith, By hearing ye shall hear, and shall not understand; and seeing ye shall see, and shall not perceive:*
> *Mat. 13:15 For this* <u>people's</u> (Israel) <u>heart is waxed gross, and their ears are dull of hearing, and their eyes they have closed; lest at any time they should see with their eyes, and hear with their ears, and should understand with their heart, and should be converted, and I should heal them.</u>

In a nutshell, Jesus is telling Israel that their understanding and perception could not be an accomplishment of their own wills and intellect. This truth applies to all humankind. God controls the Garden gate, ark doors, language creations, nation creations, and even the understanding of men, by the power of His will alone. Why, then, did God even bother to put them under the Law?

In Romans and Galatians, Paul reveals the law for what its real purpose was; it was not salvation:

> *Rom 3:20 Therefore* ___*by the deeds of the law there*___
> ___*shall no flesh be justified*___ *in his sight: for* ___*by the law*___
> ___*is the knowledge of sin.*___
> *Gal 2:16 Knowing that a man is not justified by the*
> *works of the law, but by the faith of Jesus Christ,*
> *even we have believed in Jesus Christ, that we might*
> *be justified by the faith of Christ, and not by the*
> *works of the law: for* ___*by the works of the law shall*___
> ___*no flesh be justified*___.
> *Rom 7:7 What shall we say then?* ___*Is the law sin?*___
> ___*God forbid. Nay,*___ ___*I had not known sin, but by the*___
> ___*law*___*: for I had not known lust, except the law had*
> *said, Thou shalt not covet.*

Paul adds this detailed discourse about the purpose of the law in his letter to the Galatians.

> *Gal. 3:19* ___*Wherefore then serveth the law?*___ ___*It was*___
> ___*added because of transgressions,*___ *till the seed*
> *should come to whom the promise was made; and*
> *it was ordained by angels in the hand of a mediator.*
> *Gal. 3:21* ___*Is the law then against the promises of*___
> ___*God? God forbid*___*: for if there had been a law giv-*
> *en which could have given life, verily righteousness*
> *should have been by the law.*
> *Gal. 3:22 But the scripture hath concluded all under*
> *sin, that the promise by faith of Jesus Christ might*
> *be given to them that believe.*

*Gal. 3:23 But **before faith came, we were kept under the law,** shut up unto the faith which should af-
terwards be revealed.*

*Gal. 3:24 Wherefore **the law was our schoolmaster
to bring us unto Christ, that we might be justified
by faith.***

*Gal. 3:25 But after that faith is come, we are no lon-
ger under a schoolmaster.*

God was not contradicting Himself. Law-keeping seemed to
offer hope. But it preceded the truth of salvation by faith alone.
The Law was pictured, as a "schoolmaster" to teach man the
deeper truth of salvation by grace alone. As far as any possibility of salvation by this "schoolmaster", it was a subtle, but very
real, "fixed gulf", established to bring mankind to the only bridge
to heaven. The way to this bridge was finally revealed through
Paul. The best summation of this new "way" is found in Paul's
first letter to the Corinthians. Precisely stated, salvation comes
through belief in the gospel of the death, burial, and resurrection
of Jesus Christ

*1 Cor. 15:1 Moreover, brethren, I declare unto you
the gospel which I preached unto you, which also ye
have received, and wherein ye stand;*

*1 Cor. 15:2 **By which also ye are saved**, if ye keep
in memory what I preached unto you, unless ye have
believed in vain.*

*1 Cor. 15:3 For I delivered unto you first of all that
which I also received, **how that Christ died** for our
sins according to the scriptures;*

*1 Cor. 15:4 And that **he was buried**, and that **he
rose again the third day** according to the scriptures:*

Again, someone might ask, "Why did God create the inter-
vening step of obedience to the Law?" "Why didn't He directly
teach man about grace and forgo the subtle illusion of salvation
by the law?" Again, I submit that God knew that this was a lesson
necessary to expose the inability of any man to earn or achieve
his salvation. He knew that man needed to learn this by experience. Inevitably, children won't learn some truths of life until
they experience it firsthand; for instance, the truth about fire, or
a sign that says "wet paint". Likewise, men had to be shown that
their law-keeping could not bridge the "gulf" that has separated
them from God ever since their sin in the Garden of Eden. Israel
did not see this. They burned (crucified) their only bridge to
salvation, even after being constantly told about the promised
Messiah by their prophets. If you review the Old Testament history of Israel after they received the law, you will find a continual cycle of their pious promising to obey; followed by a repeated
failure to obey; followed by punishment for their failures; followed by a national repentance to return to the promise to obey;
and then, inevitably, a repetition of this cycle.

It is important to understand that Israel's history of failure
did not affect their place as God's chosen people. Israel is still
God's chosen nation to whom there are, as yet, promises of God
awaiting fulfillment. God will never leave His promises unful-
filled. But, Israel's history stands as living historical proof that
the law could not save.

The whole script of God: calling out a people for himself;
bringing them out of bondage; giving them the land promised
to them; delivering them from their enemies; giving them kings;
giving them the moral, ceremonial and civil law to governed by;
giving them the promise of a Messiah, who was to be the King
of the promised kingdom; promising them salvation in this kingdom under this King; finally putting this promised Messiah in
their midst, only to have Him rejected and crucified, was a script
written and fulfilled for the purpose of the perfect display of the

grace that is required to perfectly, and justly, provide salvation to any man. The fulfillment of all God's promises were temporarily interrupted by the "subtle, fixed gulf" of the law. But, the giving of the Law was not without a purpose. The Law served God's purpose rather than thwarting it. This winding trail of Jewish history revealed the need for another "way" of salvation.

Here is an account of where Israel was taught this lesson. In the gospels of Matthew, Mark and Luke, there is a description of the occasion when Jesus was approached by a rich ruler who boasted to Him about his law-keeping but left in sorrow because he would not part with his wealth to follow Jesus. Jesus then taught the disciples how hard it was for a man to get to heaven by using the analogy of the camel going through a needle. Here is the story as told by Matthew:

> *Mat 19:24 And again I say unto you, It is easier for a camel to go through the eye of a needle, than for a rich man to enter into the kingdom of God.*

This response of Jesus was not just a warning against the danger of riches. The rich young ruler also thought he was "qualified for eternal life" because of his personal "law-keeping". Jesus exposed his "law-keeping" poverty by revealing the real treasure of his heart – his wealth. This teaching was a jolt to the disciples, who lived in a "law-keeping" mindset. The salvation impossibility implied by this analogy, caused them to ask the pertinent question Jesus had to be glad to hear:

> *Mat 19:25 When his disciples heard it, they were exceedingly amazed, saying,* **_Who then can be saved?_**

The implication of the impossibility of law-keeping salvation, realized by the disciples, was their equivalent to my introductory allegory about the traveling salesman, who finally understands the old farmer's statement of, "You can't get there from here." The salesman's next question would have been, "Well, then how can I get there?" This same question by the disciples implies their realization of the fact that the way they thought would secure their entrance to the kingdom of God – law-keeping – was a dead-end path. Comprehending this truth led them to plead, *"Who then can be saved?"*

Even though the deeper truth, that only Jesus can open anyone's heart to this truth through the regenerating work of the Spirit, had yet to be revealed, Jesus had to be pleased with this question from His disciples. Their question of, *"Who then can be saved?"*, was one of the first glimmers of understanding given to them. It led to their grasping of the narrowness of the way of salvation. But, the full truth of how any man receives the gift of faith that leads to salvation is subsequently revealed to men through the Spirit-inspired writings of the apostle Paul, where he unveils the complete mystery of God's sequential works that are essential for every salvation. (These works are detailed in Part 2, Topic 8.)

Back to the issue of Israel being separated by the "subtle, fixed gulf" of the law, it may seem like I'm stretching the point, but I stand behind it. The rich man in Hell; Adam and Eve locked out of Eden; and all the people shut out of the ark, shared a common experience. They were all made well aware of how God sovereignly controls any access to Himself (i.e. salvation). In contrast, Israel did not see the Law for the "gulf" that it truly was. The Law appeared to Israel as a means to salvation and reconciliation with God, but it was, in reality, a "salvation mirage" that appealed to their human pride. Did Israel ever think they could satisfy God through the Law? Yes. Did God ever think or hope that they could ever meet His required standard of perfect obedience? No, because, *"known to Him are all His works"*, including the necessity of the atoning work of His Son, Jesus Christ, by His incarnation, earthly ministry, shed blood, death, burial, and resurrection. Nevertheless, the sacrifice of "his only begotten Son" should not be seen as a last-ditch effort by God to redeem men. It was a foreordained work of God.

> *1 Pet. 1:18 Forasmuch as ye know that **ye were not redeemed with corruptible things**, as silver and gold, from your vain conversation received by tradition from your fathers;*
> *1 Pet. 1:19 **But with the precious blood of Christ**, as of a lamb without blemish and without spot:*
> *1 Pet. 1:20 **Who verily was foreordained before the foundation of the world**, but was manifest in these last times for you,*

CHAPTER 8

A Review of Six, Earthly "Fixed Gulfs"

THERE IS A SEVENTH "fixed gulf", yet to be discussed. It could be the most misapprehended, or at least disbelieved, of all of the previously noted "fixed gulfs" created by God. However, before exploring the details of this final "fixed gulf", a brief review of the previous six "fixed gulfs" is offered to reset the perspective of the "fixed gulf" operation of God in His relationship with mankind.

In His creation, God is a boundary setter. He separates heaven and earth, the ocean from the shore, sets the reproductive boundaries among animal kinds, etc., to name just a few examples of His ordained boundaries. The "fixed gulf" revealed in Luke chapter 16 is a literal, and permanent, example of the principle of separation that God must maintain between Himself and sinful man. The previous six "gulfs" (boundaries) all reflect this principle.

The first explicit declaration of the term "fixed gulf", was revealed by Jesus in the 16th chapter of the gospel of Luke. The tormented rich man, residing in the destination of all unbelievers, did not understand the degree of separation it represented. In answer to the rich man's request of Abraham to send Lazarus with a drop of water for relief, Abraham revealed the irreversibility of his situation and the impossibility of any relief from his torment. The terrifying status of the rich man was a glimpse of Hell, which Jesus shared with His disciples. It was a vivid description of both the eternal torment or the eternal rest, which awaits all men, depending upon their belief or unbelief. The expression of this separation between these two ordained destinations is precisely defined in the phrase "*great gulf fixed*" (Luke 16:26). The Luke account is the first and only literal expression about a "fixed gulf" in Scripture. It is a God-ordained boundary of separation.

The underlying truth about the "*great gulf fixed*" of Luke 16 is that, at its core, it represents a God-created separation between himself and sin. Of all of His creation, only angels and men were capable of sin. Water, rocks, earth, plants, and all other components of God's creation all are incapable of sin. Nevertheless, God's initial curse for sin fell on all of creation as well as the fallen angels and all humanity. However, the eternal "*great gulf fixed*" is a judgment for only the lost angels and men who die in sin. Sin is the only reason for death.

The "*great gulf fixed*" is a real "gulf" that exists in the real afterlife realm. However, it is not the only demonstration of a God-ordained act of separation to be experienced by mankind. In addition to the "*great gulf fixed*" in Luke 16, there are five other discernable "fixed gulfs" which were examined in Part 1 of this book.

The gate of Eden was the first "fixed (uncrossable) "gulf" (boundary) that was examined. It is also the first demonstration of God's sovereign denial of any possible willful action by man to gain (or re-gain) his lost eternal life. Whether Adam and Eve ever gave a thought about re-entry to the Garden is not known. I dare to say that the moment they encountered the world outside Eden's gate, re-entry looked very desirable. However, the expulsion of the man and woman by the Godhead through an eastern gate of the Garden, coupled with the guardianship of Cherubims and a flaming sword, created an unmistakable "fixed gulf" that barred any possible re-entry. There was no doubt about the irreversibility of this expulsion.

> Gen. 3:24 *So he drove out the man; and he placed at the east of the garden of Eden Cherubims, and a flaming sword which turned every way, to keep the way of the tree of life.*

Chronologically, the next "gulf" revealed is in the denied access to salvation via Noah's ark. The hearts of lost men, by a natural course, had grown so evil that God sentenced the earth and all of its inhabitants to destruction by a worldwide flood. Only Noah, his wife, his three sons, and their wives were saved by God's grace and their obedience in building and filling the ark as directed by God. God's sovereign will was displayed through the obedience of Noah's faith (Heb. 11:7). However, Noah's faith had to be a "gift" of God like all acts of saving faith (Eph. 2:8-9). Otherwise, God would have been showing "respect" to Noah for something he did or was. God's grace saved Noah and his family from this earthly display of God's judgment for sin. Later, Scripture reveals the real reason why Noah received the gift of faith (Eph.1:4). Noah's reprieve was a prototype demonstration of God's work of election. The divinely "shut door" was another visual evidence, of God's sovereign denial of salvation to unbelieving men.

The next act of divine separation taken by God was the "gulf" that thwarted the conspiracy of the tower of Babel builders. God applied a supernatural imposition of different languages upon mankind, which resulted in their forced dispersal over the earth.

It is interesting to imagine what was the immediate reaction of all those men, who could no longer communicate with each other. This event became the source of the descriptive word for confusing speech - "babel". But, to the dismay of many linguists, there was no language "evolution" that occurred. The creation of diverse languages among men was an obvious and instantaneous intervention by God because of a disobedient scheme of men. It was as spontaneous as were the spoken acts of creation, as documented in Genesis 1. Read again, the account of the incident as recorded in Genesis 11.

> *Gen. 11:6 And the LORD said, Behold, the people is one, and <u>they have all one language; and this they begin to do: and now nothing will be restrained from them, which they have imagined to do.</u>*
> *Gen. 11:7 Go to,* **<u>let us go down, and there confound their language</u>***<u>, that they may not understand one another's speech.</u>*
> *Gen. 11:8 So the <u>LORD scattered them abroad from thence upon the face of all the earth</u>: and they left off to build the city.*

God did not need an "evolutionary" period to elapse for the "scattering" to occur. Between verses 7 and 8, the language "gulf" was instantly imposed upon all mankind.

As history progressed, the next "gulf" occurred when God imposed another boundary among humanity by forming a chosen people (nation) through one man, Abraham, and his descendants. At the opening of Chapter 12 of Genesis, out of all the inhabitants of the world's population, God sovereignly chose to communicate with a pagan man, Abram. Abram was a man who had no distinctive virtues that would warrant God's choice of him. There is no record of God thinking, "Oh, I think this man

Abram will believe me or, I detect a grain of faith in this man, so I'll make the offer to him."

The result of all of the promises made to Abraham was that all of God's subsequent, direct communications with mankind would be limited to Abraham and his descendant race of people through Isaac - the Jews. All Gentiles (all non-Jews), with the exclusion of a small number of later proselytes, were shut out from any direct communications or blessings from God. Furthermore, the Gentiles, by their state of enmity with God, were contentedly unconcerned about this God created "gulf" of separation. They willingly preferred their pagan gods and idols.

This God-ordained, preferential creation of, and treatment of the Jews, created a subtle, but real separation from other men. It may have seemed inconsequential at first, but through the course of Jewish history, it became increasingly evident. God had placed the "light" of His blessings on Israel. True to the Biblical principle of darkness hating the light, the Gentile world has proceeded to hate Israel ever since. The world's continued hatred of Israel to this day is one of the best testimonies of fallen man's enmity with God. No ethnic group is more hated than the Jews. While this God-created "gulf" began quietly (subtly), it was confirmed by an obvious and instinctive racial hatred among the nations of the world as history progressed. The continued existence of this ancient race, coupled with the relentless, universal persecution of them, is a double testimony to the fact that the Jews and their continued existence are a miracle work of God.

With God's relationship with man narrowed to His chosen people, the next "gulf" (boundary) set is the Law, which was given by God to Israel for its governance and worship. This gulf is also a "subtle" one, because the unperceived inability of any person to perfectly meet the requirements of the Law. The "gulf" represented by the Law was not immediately perceptible to Israel. Israel never objected to the receiving of any of the specific Law commands from God. God even went so far as to acknowledge in advance, their future failings of law-keeping by instituting a system of sacrifices for Israel to perform when they failed to keep the law. (However, these sacrifices could only atone for an individual's temporal sins. None of man's God-prescribed system of sacrifices could pay for the inherent sin of all men from their being "in Adam".)

Man's moral inability to satisfactorily meet the demands of the Law revealed a "fixed gulf" (a yoke). Even though no part of the Law was unachievable by man, no one could attain salvation by their perfect obedience to the Law by means of their own will. In Romans 3, Paul proceeded to show that all the world (Israel and Gentile) was guilty under the law.

> *Rom. 3:19 Now we know that <u>what things soever the law saith,</u> it saith to them who are under the law: that every mouth may be stopped, **and <u>all the world may become guilty before God.</u>***

Paul points out that the law "stops the mouth" of two groups; both the Jews and the rest of the world (Gentiles). If "the Law" left Israel guilty, then all those apart from it (all Gentiles) are hopelessly guilty. It makes the whole world guilty. The Law is a "moral mirror" that exposes the truth of the sin of every person.

> *Rom. 3:23 <u>For all have sinned, and come short of the glory of God</u>;*

Part 1 has been a review of six "gulfs" that God has placed between Himself and mankind. They are all acts of separation to restrain man's access to God in demonstration of His sovereignty. This sets the stage for a final "fixed gulf" to be examined. It is a "fixed gulf" that has afflicted mankind ever since their fall into sin in the Garden of Eden. This final "gulf" was a component of each of the prior six "gulfs" in this discussion. However, as a stand-alone "gulf", it is still generally unacknowledged within Christendom. This "fixed gulf" is built upon a flawed presumption about the role of man's will in his salvation. It will be the focus of Part 2 of this book.

The Final "Fixed Gulf" The Fact of, and the Illusion of, "Free Will"

IF THE TITLE ABOVE of Part 2 strikes you as slightly oxymoronic, it has a purpose. Regarding the factual aspect of "free will", it is an imperative demanded by God's justice. Any dispensing of punishment by God for a violation of His Law is incumbent upon a person's responsibility to obey, which, in turn, requires that every person must be able to obey. Therefore, the crucial aspect of one's obedience is their possession of a free, "un-incumbered" will by which to choose to obey or disobey. Since the Bible is explicit about the truth that anyone who dies in unbelief will receive an eternal condemnation to hell from Christ, the judge of all the earth (Gen. 18:25), it necessitates the truth that all humanity must possess a totally "un-incumbered" free will at some moment in time. The question that eludes many Christians is question of, "When, in all of history, did all men possess this attribute of pure free will that the proper application of Divine judgment requires? The Biblical answer to this critical question will be exposited later in Topic 11 of Part 2. This explains the factual aspect of the title above.

The illusion aspect arises from how one defines the term free will. As was noted in Part 1, the perception that people still have a free will has always played a part in God's "fixed gulfs". If by the term free will, it is suggested that every man is able to make all of his or her choices according to whatever his or her will desires, then the definition of "free will" is still true. Man is free to do what he or she wants, within their particular physical, environmental and moral constraints. The will of man is the driving force behind every choice a person makes. However, if one's definition of free will insists on the assertion that no other external power exerts any influence upon a man's will, then the concept of free will is false.

The following two verses confirm that men instinctively do what "seems" right to them.

> *Jdg. 21:25 In those days there was no king in Israel:*
> *every man did that which was **right in his own eyes.***

When man disconnected himself from being under God's authority in Eden, this became the new attitude that guided all of his decisions. The concept of free will was mankind's perceived reality (truth), but the way that "seems" right to mankind is eternally fatal. Proverbs 16:25 confirms this truth.

> *Prov. 16:25 There is a way that **seemeth right** unto*
> *a man, but the end thereof are the ways of death.*

In the post-Eden days, Adam did not realize that, by yielding to Satan's temptation in the Garden, he had foolishly put himself under a new authority that would become a natural influencer of all his choices. Adam knew that by God's authority, he had

been expelled from the Garden, but the new internal controlling influence of Satan was unperceived. Men's belief that they
still have a "free will" is merely an illusion that Satan effectively
employs to keep men in rebellion against God, by continuing
to act as "their own gods" (Gen. 3:5). This was the result of the
spiritual death that fell on all mankind, unless, and until, God's
grace rescues (saves) them.

For this reason, I assert that the concept of free will has both
a true and a false context. It "was" a reality (true) in man, as God
created him, but ever since man's fall in Eden, it is "now" an illusion (false). The Part 1 discussion of some of the "fixed gulfs"
of Scripture has set the stage for the investigation of the seventh
"fixed gulf". The subsequent topics presented in Part 2 will attempt to put this final gulf in perspective.

Immediately prior to Christ's departure from His earthly
ministry, the promised kingdom of God was on the mind of his
disciples.

> *Acts 1:6 When they therefore were come together,
> they asked of him, saying, <u>Lord, wilt thou at this
> time restore again the kingdom to Israel?</u>*

After Christ's ascension, the gospel of the kingdom continued to be proclaimed by the apostles to Israel. The essence of
that particular gospel is clearly proclaimed by Peter in verses 37
and 38 of Acts 2. His audience was distinctly noted in Acts 2:14
as being the "men of Judea" (Israelites). When the men of Israel
realized their error and their guilt for having crucified Jesus, it
prompted a question from them. They received a clear answer
from Peter in verse 38.

> *Acts 2:37 Now when they heard this, they were
> pricked in their heart, and said unto Peter and to the*

*rest of the apostles, Men and brethren, **what shall***
we do?
*Acts 2:38 Then Peter said unto them, **Repent**, and*
be baptized** every one of you **in the name of Jesus
***Christ** for the remission of sins, and ye shall receive*
the gift of the Holy Ghost.

To acquire forgiveness there were the three "works" required of Israel for salvation:

1. *Repent* – an internal, mental acknowledgment of their guilt in rejecting and crucifying Jesus and the desire to turn from it.
2. *be baptized* – a law commanded, literal, physical act of cleansing, which was of particular importance to Israel because of the prophecy of Exodus 19:6. This prophecy foretold that Israel would become a kingdom of priests. The future result of that prophecy would require that every Israelite in this kingdom would have to undergo priestly cleansing in preparation for their priestly assignment. Numbers Chapters 8 and 19 provide a detailed account of God's requirement for cleansing and purifying of priests.
3. *in the name of Jesus Christ* – the specific context for baptism is one that acknowledged that the man, Jesus, whom they crucified, was the Christ, the anointed Son of God, the promised Messiah of Israel, upon whose return, the Kingdom will be established, and when Israel will assume their priestly role.

The promised results of obedience by Israel of the three "works" above would be *the remission of sins*, (salvation) and the *the gift of the Holy Spirit* that is the seal of salvation given for their obedience..

Despite Peter's sermon, Israel, as a nation, continued in their rejection of their Messiah, culminating with the stoning of Stephen (Acts 8). But there was a remnant of Jews who believed. They formed the early "Jewish church" as documented in Acts 1: 13-15. This "church" was not the "church" that Paul reveals as the "body of Christ (Col. 1:24). The *church* of Acts 1 was a church of Jewish believers who were still under the law, in contrast to the "body of Christ" which is not under law, but rather was under grace (Rom. 6:14). The stoning of Stephen by unbelieving Jews became the incident where God began His introduction of a new dispensation with a new gospel message.

This new gospel would be introduced by Christ's choosing, saving of, and commissioning of, Saul of Tarsus to be His messenger. The new gospel was the offer of salvation by "faith alone", to any man, Jew or Gentile, who would believe in the life, death, burial, and resurrection of the Son of God – Jesus Christ, *according to the Scriptures.* Saul, who was renamed Paul, stresses the truth of salvation by "faith". It is a word he mentions 34 times in his letter to the Romans. However, this new gospel, given from the ascended Lord, through Paul, would also become a gospel that contained a new, but not readily understood, "fixed gulf".

In all of the previous "gulfs", it was shown how God divinely separated Himself from any access by any actions of man's "supposed" free will. What differentiates the previous "gulfs" from the "fixed gulf" of the new dispensation of grace is that men, in prior dispensations, were made aware, either immediately or eventually, of the fact that no willful act could overcome the obstacles which these previous "fixed gulfs" presented to them. Adam and Eve knew that they could not "will" their re-entry to Eden. When the flood overwhelmed all those outside the ark, they knew their wills were useless to save them. When the tower conspirators of Babel found themselves instantly unable to communicate verbally, their only willful option was to scatter. When God constricted his blessings to Abraham and his descendants, all people outside of Israel, (Gentiles) knew that God had separated Israel from the all other nations. When the nation of Israel eventually experienced their inability to perfectly keep the Law by their history of failures to do so, they experienced the inability of their wills to overcome their deficiency. Whether these "gulfs" were immediately perceived or were eventually understood, the will of man was revealed as helpless to conquer any of them.

However, in this dispensation of grace, where the required step to salvation is simply "belief in the gospel", the inadequacy of man's "free will" to meet this requirement is still greatly misunderstood. Part 2 of this book willl focus on revealing the fact that this "free will gulf" is still operative.

To prove the fact of this "gulf", two Biblical realities must be recognized. First, the Biblical distinctiveness of this current dispensation of grace from the previous dispensation of Law, must be understood. Part of the obstacle for many Christians to their understanding of this distinction is the fact that the distinct dispensation of grace did not begin until Acts, Chapter 9, where God chose and saved the apostle Paul. If God's choice and saving of Paul are properly understood, it reveals the proper context of the four gospels and the first eight chapters of Acts as remaining correctly set in the dispensation of Law. The context of the dispensation of the Law is Jewish. The major distinction of the dispensation of Law, from the dispensation of grace, is that the gospel of the Law dispensation required salvation by faith plus works. The previous exposition of Acts 2:38 above confirms the works requirement.

A second distinction that separates the law and grace dispensations is the fact that, apart from becoming a proselyte of Judaism, there was no Gentile hope for salvation, before the new gospel of salvation by "faith alone" was revealed. In the new dispensation of grace, salvation is now available to both Jew and Gentile without distinction.

Rom 3:22 righteousness of God by faith of Jesus Christ towards all, and upon all those who believe: for there is no difference;

Rom 10:12 For there is no difference of Jew and Greek; for the same Lord of all is rich towards all that call upon him.

Unfortunately, much of Christianity still studies, preaches and teaches the entire New Testament in a unified, Christian context. The distinction between these two dispensations is generally ignored in the doctrinal teachings and creeds of most churches and Christian denominations today. The failure to distinguish between these two dispensations results in the inevitable blending of the elements of the law into the doctrinal creeds and practices of Christians in this age of grace. This "blending" intuitively produces the spirit of legalism. Any degree of legalism in belief leads people to conclude that their salvation, and/ or eternal security, depends upon some degree of the self-discipline of their will, which thereby detracts from the purity and scope of the grace of God in their salvation. Law and grace are antithetical. Paul clearly announces the context of the new dispensation of grace for believers.

*Rom. 6:14 For sin shall not have dominion over you: for **ye are not under the law, but under grace**.*

By the Damascus road conversion of Christianity's most avowed enemy, Saul of Tarsus, God began a new dispensation of His redemptive purpose among mankind. The essence of the gospel for this new dispensation was that the offer of salvation was now open to all men, without distinction, by faith alone. The ascended, glorified Christ would reveal to Paul (Saul) that, henceforth, no conversion to Judaism, no law-keeping and no works of any kind by man, could produce, or even help to produce, salvation. All that is required of men is their belief in the gospel that Paul was directly commissioned, by Christ, to preach.

> *1 Cor. 15:1* Moreover, brethren, __I declare unto you the gospel which I preached unto you__,...
> *1 Cor. 15:2* __By which also ye are saved__, *if ye keep in memory what I preached unto you, unless ye have believed in vain.*
> *1 Cor. 15:3 For I delivered unto you first of all that which I also received,* __how that Christ died for our sins according to the scriptures;__
> *1 Cor. 15:4 And that he was buried, and that he rose again the third day* __according to the scriptures:__

This is all that had to be believed for salvation. This path to salvation was as simple as it can get, right?; or was it?

The mode of this offer of the gospel of salvation appears unambiguous and straightforward. It is to be presented to all men, without distinction, for their willful acceptance or rejection. This offer is so openly made, that it is equivalent to a hypothetical act of God reopening the gates of the Garden of Eden and allowing "whosoever will" to enter and partake of the Tree of Life. But, given the Scriptural fact that God has already chosen from before the foundation of the world, all of whom He will save, He could never allow a non-elect (non-chosen) person to believe by an act of his or her (presumed) "free will"?

Because God "knows all His works from the beginning" (Acts 15:18), there is no possibility that a non-elect person might gain salvation by his or her "free will". God knows the "dominion" and the spiritual death-grip that sin holds over every unbeliever. God also knows all whom He will set free from that dominion through His gift of faith, by grace alone, according to His will alone. The truth of whom He has chosen, resides in God's sovereign knowledge alone. God has His secrets, and He only reveals what He wills, to whom He wills (Deut. 29:29)(Rom. 9:16 & Exo. 33:19). The knowledge of those who are to be the recipients of the gift of saving faith is one of His secrets.

Nevertheless, the terms of this new offer of salvation became the most obtainable offer yet in the minds of men. At the outset of the dispensation of the grace of God (*Eph. 3:2 If ye have heard of the dispensation of the grace of God which is given me to you-ward*), with such a simple gospel requirement, there were now, no apparent "fixed gulfs" in view that could hinder mankind's access to God. With no ethnic or law barriers in view in this new dispensation, salvation is now made available by merely "believing the gospel". This should be no problem because belief is something anyone can do.

But, by God's allowance, Satan has successfully exploited the illusion of "free will" to delude men in believing in their ability to choose to believe for salvation. This illusion has remained as an imperceptible "fixed gulf" to men. Although all of Adam's descendants were spiritually dead, man's ability to reason and make choices produces the logical conclusion that saving faith is now merely a personal action that is entirely within every man's capability. In turn, the delusion about man's capacity to believe, placed the burden of responsibility on every individual person, to respond to the repeated calls in the New Testament for men to believe the gospel. But, what a large portion of Christianity has failed to discern are two God-created, God-purposed truths that seem to be in open contradiction:

1. the Scriptural command of men to believe the gospel for salvation, (1 Cor. 15:1-4), (Rom. 10:9), seemingly contradicted by....

2. the revealed mystery of natural man's inability to discern "spiritual things" (1 Cor. 2:14), because of his spiritual state of being "*dead in sins and trespasses*'. (Eph. 2:1)

An alert skeptic of these two points might object and plead that their very "inability to believe" is grounds for their pardon from any condemnation for their disbelief. Objection overruled. 1 Cor. 2:14 denies the very possibility for the unbeliever to ever spiritually "know" of his inability to discern *the things of the Spirit of God*". They cannot object to a truth they cannot discern.

> *1 Cor. 2:14 But the <u>natural man receiveth not the things of the Spirit of God</u>: for they are foolishness unto him: <u>neither **can** he know them, **because they are spiritually discerned.**</u>*

This verse will be cited often in the Topics that follow. It openly denies the possibility of a natural (sinful) man making the necessary spiritual discernment that might lead to a "free will" decision to believe. Note the phrase, "...*neither can he know them*,...". Paul is writing about something natural man "can't know", not "won't know". If there is something a man can't possibly do, such as fly like a bird, or live underwater like the fish, then no degree of a man's will can make it happen. If the discernment about one's helpless bondage in sin, and about the sufficiency of Christ's offer of salvation, don't qualify as revelations of the "*things of the Spirit of God*", I don't know what does. The ability of "*natural man*" to discern such "*things*" was lost in Eden.

If the Scriptures are rightly understood, they expose the inability of man's will, to even "believe" the gospel, apart from God's regenerative salvation works in them. Many people reject these progressively revealed truths. They reason, if man cannot use his free will to believe, then it would be "unfair" for a "just" God to condemn anyone for something he or she cannot do. True, but the crucial point the rejecters overlook is the fact that man, "as he was created", had the ability to "believe". The topics of "belief" and "fairness " will be examined below, but first, the role of the works of man needs to be considered.

On the following page, there is an illustration of how 1 Corinthians 2:14 is perhaps, one of the best scriptural validations of the existence of a "fixed gulf" that God has put between himself and sinful man. After this illustration, the remainder of Part 2 of this book will be devoted to presentation of a variety of topics that are aimed at dissecting and corroborating the realities of man's separated position from God and the necessary comprehension of *things of the Spirit of God* that are required for any man to cross this "gulf".

If this verse is true..........

*1 Cor. 2:14 But the natural man receiveth not the **things of the Spirit of God**, for they are foolishness unto him: neither can he know them, because they are spiritually discerned.*

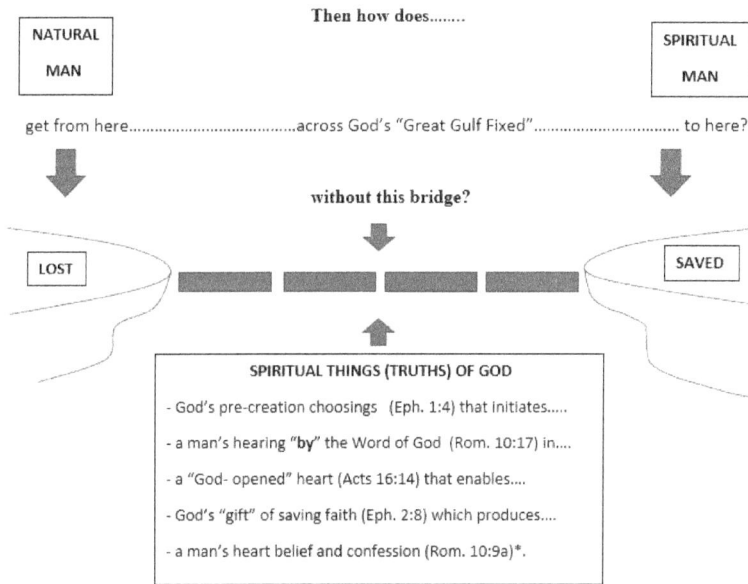

Then how does........

| NATURAL MAN | | SPIRITUAL MAN |

get from here...........................across God's "Great Gulf Fixed"................................ to here?

without this bridge?

LOST

SAVED

SPIRITUAL THINGS (TRUTHS) OF GOD

- God's pre-creation choosings (Eph. 1:4) that initiates.....

- a man's hearing "**by**" the Word of God (Rom. 10:17) in....

- a "God- opened" heart (Acts 16:14) that enables....

- God's "gift" of saving faith (Eph. 2:8) which produces....

- a man's heart belief and confession (Rom. 10:9a)*.

The answer is: He cannot get "there" except by the "will of God". John 1:13

(For those who reject the universality of the Scriptural salvation sequence above, they must produce some other Scriptural explanation(s) of the reason how and why men are saved, keeping in mind that God is not a "respecter of persons".)

(* While Rom. 10:9b specifies belief in the death and resurrection of the Lord Jesus, all salvations prior to that event would require belief in whatever gospel God had provided in their particular time of existence; i.e. Abel, Noah, Abraham, Isaac, Jacob, Joseph, Moses, Rahab, David, Mary, John the Baptist, the twelve disciples, etc. The same salvation sequence had to be applied to all these notable people. Although their required gospel obedience differed, the saving sequence, that was applied to them and brought them to faith, did not, and could not vary from the "Truths" above, lest God was, in some way, "respecting" of them.)

Topic 1. The Place of Work(s) in Theology

Before I expound upon the hidden "fixed gulf" of this new dispensation and its gospel, attention needs to be given to the concept of "work" and its contextual use in the theological sense. The noun "work" has a crucial part to play in both the previous "gulf" of the law and the new "gulf" of the dispensation of grace, that followed the dispensation of law. If Scripture is not carefully and rightly divided, there is a real tension created between how Paul defines justification and how James, the brother of Christ, the leader of the early Jewish Christian church, defines justification, with regards to the subject of "work(s)". Listen to Paul's concise definition of how justification happens and does not happen:

> Gal. 2:16 <u>Knowing that **a man is not justified**</u>
> <u>**by the works of the law**</u>, but <u>by the faith of Jesus</u>

> *Christ, even we have believed in Jesus Christ, that*
> *we might be justified by the faith of Christ, and not*
> *by the works of the law: for by the works of the law*
> *shall no flesh be justified*

Now read James' contradictory definition of justification.

> *Jas. 2:20 But wilt thou know, O vain man, **that faith***
> ***without works is dead**?*
> *Jas. 2:21 Was not Abraham our father justified by*
> *works, when he had offered Isaac his son upon the*
> *altar?*
> *Jas. 2:22 Seest thou how faith wrought with his*
> *works, and by works was faith made perfect?*
> *Jas. 2:23 And the scripture was fulfilled which saith,*
> *Abraham believed God, and it was imputed unto*
> *him for righteousness: and he was called the Friend*
> *of God.*
> *Jas. 2:24 Ye see then how that **by works a man is***
> ***justified, and not by faith only.***

The proper exposition of this apparent contradiction is dependent upon the correct contextual placement of each statement. Paul is writing about the pre-salvation context of every human being. He is explaining the utter inability of any *"works of the law"* to achieve a man's justification in the eyes of God. In contrast, James was writing to the dispersed, believing Jews of Israel (Jas. 1:1), in accord with the revised commission which he and the other eleven apostles agreed to at the Council of Jerusalem. Paul recorded the new agreement in Galatians.

> *Gal. 2:9 And when James, Cephas, and John, who*
> *seemed to be pillars, perceived the grace that was*
> *given unto me, they gave to me and Barnabas the*

*right hands of fellowship; that we should go unto the heathen, and **they** (James, Cephas, and John) **unto the circumcision**.*

James 2:24 above was written in a post-salvation context to a Jewish audience. James was teaching that the evidence of salvation in any of his Jewish audience must be revealed through their "works" (obedience). Recall Peter's new gospel, proclaimed in Acts 2:38, to Israel, still in the dispensation of the Law.

> *Acts 2:38 Then Peter said unto them, Repent, and be baptized every one of you in the name of Jesus Christ for the remission of sins, and ye shall receive the gift of the Holy Ghost.*

Every Jew, who believed and complied with this gospel command, would receive the gift of the Holy Spirit. But a fact that is largely unrecognized is that Israel's obligation to keep the Law of Moses remained in effect, even after their resurrected Messiah ascended to heaven. After the ascension, obedience to the Law would continue until *"every one of you"* (all Israel) was saved. Only then, could the saved nation of Israel evangelize the other nations of the earth. But, this did not happen at that time. The redemption (salvation) of the elect of Israel will be accomplished in the prophesied Great Tribulation. In the Millenium, their evangelistic mission will be carried out. In keeping with the mutually agreed decision of the Council of Jerusalem, James, Cephas (Peter), and John directed their ministries and the gospel of Acts 2:38 towards Israel.

Consequently, the epistles they penned are written directly to their fellow Jews. This is the stated context in which James wrote, as is stated in James 1:1:

> *Jas. 1:1 James, a servant of God and of the Lord Jesus Christ, **to the twelve tribes** which are scattered abroad, greeting.*

Thus, putting James 2:20-24 in the correct context, James is saying that the lack of any external evidence of faith means there must be no faith or "dead faith" in a person. The nation Israel was born and raised in a work's context in the dispensation of the Law. James, a half-brother of Jesus and the acknowledged leader of the early church of Jewish believers, was, in this post-resurrection letter, trying to shift the Jewish "works mindset" into a new context. The context of works was well known to believing Jews. Works would now become signs (external evidence) of salvation, instead of a futile path to attain salvation.

As previously noted, Peter acknowledged that *"we"* (the Jews) would be saved by faith just as *"they"* (Gentiles) were – that is by "faith alone".

> *Acts 15:11 But we believe that through the grace of the Lord Jesus Christ **we** (Jews) **shall be saved, even as they** (Gentiles).*

Paul likewise confirmed the importance of, and the place of, works in all those saved "by faith".

> *Eph. 2:10 For we are his workmanship, **created in Christ Jesus unto good works**, which God hath before ordained that we **should walk** in them.*

Take particular note of the verb tense *"should walk"* in this verse. The context of James' teaching was about works in the life of Jewish believers. There is no context of "should walk" in James' letter.

A Great Gulf Fixed

However, in the age of grace it is imporant to remember that not all believers will produce the same amount of works. Scripture affirms that different measures of faith are bestowed upon believers after their salvation. Paul makes this point:

> Rom. 12:3 For I say, through the grace given unto me, to every man that is among you, not to think of himself more highly than he ought to think; but to think soberly, __according as God hath dealt to every man the measure of faith.__

I suggest that, at the very least, every believer will produce at least one evidence (work) of their faith –their confession of belief. I think this is what Paul asserts in Romans 9.

> Rom. 10:9 That if thou shalt __confess with thy mouth the Lord Jesus__, and shalt believe in thine heart that God hath raised him from the dead, thou shalt be saved.
> Rom. 10:10 For with the heart man believeth unto righteousness; and __with the mouth confession is made unto salvation.__

Confession is a "work-evidence" of faith that comes from the heart. Verse 10 above recites the proper sequence of action between the heart and the mouth. A saving belief that originates in the heart will be testified to by the mouth of the believer. Jesus confirmed the cause and effect linkage between the heart and the mouth of a person as recorded in the gospel of Luke. It is not the mouth that puts "treasure" in the heart, but instead, the heart is the source of whatever "treasure" emerges from the mouth.

> Luke 6:45 A good man out of the good treasure of his heart bringeth forth that which is good; and an

*evil man out of the evil treasure of his heart bringeth forth that which is evil: for **of the abundance of the heart his mouth speaketh.***

In summation, both James and Paul understood works to be evidence of faith. But in Paul's ministry context, he stressed a complete disconnect between salvation and works, whereas James stressed the importance of works as an essential evidence of salvation. The difference in the focus of these two "works" contexts by Paul and James, resolve the illusion of a contradiction over the place of "works" in a believer's life.

Topic 2. Next Question - Belief - Whose Work is it?

Once the context between salvation and works is established, a deeper and more controversial question must be resolved. It is the question of, "Is the act of saving faith (belief) an independent "work" performed by lost man to gain salvation, or is it the work of God produced in the lost man?" These questions are another form of the question of, "Is man's belief a work of his free will or is it the internal work of God upon the will of a man?" It is a long-running debate among theologians. Nevertheless, it is a question that can have only one correct answer. The prime origin of saving faith cannot both "be" and "not be" a work of man.

Everyone understands the concept of faith. Believing (having faith) in something is an action that every person performs daily. From the act of riding in a car, to the act of putting a forkful of food in your mouth, both involve some degree of faith. Logic tells us that our acts of faith are self-produced by our wills. We believe the car we are riding in will safely transport us. We believe the food we are about to eat will not make us ill or kill us. Man's acts of placing faith in something, or someone, are usually based upon some prior knowledge, experience, or trust in others.

I assert that all of our daily exercises of faith are self-willed in all cases you might name, except one – saving belief (faith). Many Christians, a majority I think, philosophically contend that saving faith is also, and must be, a work of man's free will. However, in contradiction to this view, I will point to some Scriptures that refute the position which says that man's choice to believe the gospel must be, or can be, an act of his free will. These verses will support what I believe is the Biblical truth about the source of saving faith. First, look again at Galatians 2:16. Within this verse is a clear cause and effect phrase regarding how belief occurs. Note the bold type:

> *Gal. 2:16 Knowing that a man is not justified by the works of the law, <u>but **by** the faith of Jesus Christ, even we have believed **in** Jesus Christ,</u> that we might be <u>justified **by** the faith of Christ</u>, and not by the works of the law: for by the works of the law shall no flesh be justified.*

How is it we believe in Jesus? It is *"by the faith of Jesus"* (the cause) by which we (believers) *"believe in Jesus Christ"* (the effect). Those two bold type prepositions **"by"** and **"in"**, delineate a profound difference. It is standard Christian doctrine that says one must believe "in" Christ to be saved. This statement is correct, but a fact that is widely misunderstood is the mystery of "how" or "why" anyone believes "in" Christ. This mystery was not revealed until the ascended and glorified Christ revealed it through the pen of Paul. The overlooked fact of this revealed mystery was that it was *"by the faith of Christ"* that anyone is gifted with the faith to *"believe in Christ"*. I submit that the correct *"faith of"*- *"faith in"* sequence is the neglected truth embedded in Galatians 2:16 above.

It is not until the revelation of further powerful truth of Ephesians 2:8-9 that saving faith is disclosed as "the gift", that is given by grace, leading to salvation.

> *Eph. 2:8 For by **grace** are ye **saved** through **faith**;*
> *and **that** not of yourselves: **it is the gift of God**:*
> *Eph. 2:9 Not of works, lest any man should boast.*

Note that the bold type pronouns above, *that* and *it*, are singular. In the singular tense, grammatically, these two singular pronouns should only modify one of the preceding three subjects– **grace**, **saved** *(salvation)* or **faith**. Furthermore, logic dictates that only one of these nouns (subjects) can be ascribed to an individual. However, many theologians interpret either *"grace"* or *"salvation"* (saved) as the particular nouns being referred to by *"that"* and *"it"*. The interpretative choice of either one would be a superfluous revelation, because it is irrational to suppose that *"grace"* or *"salvation"* is *"of yourselves"* (or one's self). It would be pointless for Paul to tell his readers that *"grace"* or *"salvation"* was *"not of yourselves"*. In today's vernacular, the readers of Paul's letters would have responded with, "Well, duh!"

The subject of *"faith"*, however, is something that men, instinctively and logically believe, must be produced by each individual. Therefore, the significant revelation of Ephesians 2:8 focuses upon the subject of *"faith"*. It has to be the noun referenced by the pronouns *"that"* and *"it"*. This powerful passage is revealing the deep truth that saving faith itself is *"the gift of God"*. This verse defeats the idea that faith must, or can, originate in the free will of an individual. Saving faith comes through the will, but it is a will that has been divinely enlightened to belief from it's prior bondage to serve one's self.

A verse in Romans 3 is another testimony to the true cause of salvation (*the righteousness of God*).

> *Rom. 3:22 Even <u>the righteousness of God which is</u>*
> *<u>by faith of Jesus Christ unto all</u> and <u>upon all them</u>*
> *<u>that believe:</u> for there is no difference:*

Some might take this verse to portray *"all them that believe"* as the cause and the *"faith of Christ"* as the result (effect). But, any attempt from this verse to suggest, because the grammatical arrangement of this verse, that an individual's belief is the cause *"the righteousness of God"* would be in blatant contradiction to Galatians 2:16 and Ephesians 2:8-9 above.

A powerful, but very subtle passage that addresses the question of whether "belief" was a "work", in found in John, chapter 6. In verse 26, Jesus is addressing the crowd of "about five thousand" people who had just been miraculously fed. In verse 26, He rebukes them for seeking him for the sole purpose of getting more bread and fish by His miraculous power.

> *John 6:26 Jesus answered them and said, Verily, verily, I say unto you, <u>Ye seek me, not because ye saw</u>*
> *<u>the miracles, but because ye did eat of the loaves,</u>*
> *<u>and were filled</u>.*

Following this rebuke, Jesus warns them about the focus of their "labor" in verse 27.

> *John 6:27 <u>Labour not for the meat which perisheth, but for that meat which endureth unto everlasting life</u>, which the Son of man shall give unto you: for him hath God the Father sealed.*

This warning about "laboring" for the wrong thing, was cast in a "works context", which is entirely compatible with the Jewish mindset about salvation. Israel's "works mentality" was the natural outcome among these chosen people whom God had placed under the Law. When this Jewish audience heard the admonition from Jesus to adjust the focus of their "labors", the natural question in their minds was expressed logically, in plural tense, by the use of the word "works", in verse 28.

> *John 6:28 Then said they unto him,* **What shall we do, that we might work the works of God?**

It would have been logical for them to anticipate Jesus' response to contain a new "laundry list" of works (law commands) that He would expect of them. However, Jesus throws them a real, two-part change-up. First, in verse 29, we find a very subtle but profound shift in the tense of the noun "works". Jesus, does not answer them in the same plural tense with a list of "works", that they ought to be doing to obtain the "...*meat which endureth unto everlasting life...*", but instead He reveals a new profound truth by changing the verb tense from the plural, "works", to the singular noun, "work". Secondly, Jesus' revelation goes to a deeper level still, by shifting the application of the noun "work" from his audience, to God himself.

> *John 6:29 Jesus answered and said unto them,* **This is the work of God, that ye believe on him whom he hath sent.**

By this answer, Jesus has just told his audience, in one sentence, what the entire scope and purpose of God's redemptive work among mankind is. Here again, there is no expectation of, nor any responsibility of man, found in this answer to men regarding their question of, "what should we do....?" Jesus did not say, "This is the work that God says that you must do." This is a verse that requires a focus on both what is said, as well as what is not said. I contend that this profound answer by Jesus escapes the notice of many Christian pastors, theologians, and teachers.

Three other verses that put the miracle of salvation exclusively in God's hands are found in John 6, Philippians 1 and Acts 13.

> *John 6:65 And he said, Therefore said I unto you, that <u>no man can come unto me</u>, **<u>except it were given unto him</u>** of my Father.*
> *Php. 1:29 For unto you **it is given** in the behalf of Christ, not only **to believe** <u>on him</u>, but also to suffer for his sake;*
> *Acts 13:48 And when the Gentiles heard this, they were glad, and glorified the word of the Lord: and <u>as many as were</u> **ordained to eternal life** (the cause)<u> **believed**</u> (the effect).*

Only God can "give belief". When God "ordains" something to happen, it assuredly will happen.

The verses cited above, Gal. 2:16, Rom. 3:22, John 6:27-29, 1 Cor. 2:14, Php. 1:29 and Acts 13:48, form a solid defense of, and support for, the truth that the only "work" that can lead to salvation is the *"work of God"*. It is a work that is given and performed by His grace alone, to everyone chosen in accordance with His fore-ordained will (Eph. 1:4-5). But to the frustration of many Christians, the knowledge of those who are the chosen, is a secret known only to God. Believers can learn, after their salvation, of the fact that they were chosen by God before *"the foundation of the world"*. However, neither believers nor unbelievers can ever know who is a "chosen" (predestined) person, but, as yet, unsaved. Therefore, evangelism efforts must be made to reach out to all unelievers, without any presumption about whether or not a particular person is a "chosen" vessel.

If an effective spiritual effort (belief) could be performed by a lost man, apart from any help or compulsion by God, it would have to be defined as "a work of man". This means that hypothetical "free will" belief, which, by its very definition, is an act of man apart from God, would have to be understood as a "saving work". One of the foundations of Paul's message was that any work of man could have no place in their salvation.

Should it be thought that I have overreached in my interpretation of Galatians 2:16 by asserting that it is the *"faith of Christ"* that is the cause of anyone's *"faith in Christ"*, I offer a final two "if-then" arguments to refute the position that believes saving belief (faith) must be a product of a man's "free will".

1. If the "free will" position is true, then the question that must be asked is what enables "saving faith" (belief), in some, but not in others? Those who "choose to believe" must possess some level of intelligence or spiritual perception, that the others do not have. The decision to believe in Christ cannot be a random choice or a result of dumb luck. Some personal measure of intelligence or spiritual perception must be the source of one's willful decision to "believe in Christ". It would mean that they were able to perceive and process the gospel facts in their minds from which they made their decision. But no one contends that all men possess equal intelligence or equal perceptive abilities. But every Arminian (free will) apologist must produce some other logical and Biblically sound answer to this most basic question. "If your belief was a work of your free will, WHAT caused your will to believe?" or "WHY did you believe?"

2. If the "free will" position is true, then whatever the source of their choice to believe was, they were rewarded for it. God is logically obligated to save all who believe in this manner. But, if salvation is a reward for a free will choice that was made because of something in a person, then God is a "respecter of persons", obligated to respect someone's personal choice, in which He played no part. This position

fails because of the previously cited verses that assert that God is *"no respector of persons"*.

If salvation required a pure, "free will" decision to believe, then such a requirement would, in reality, be the creation of a type of New Testament, law-required "work" for salvation. Critics may run to Acts 16 and recite Paul's plain answer to the Philippian jailer's question about what he must "do" for salvation.

> *Acts 16:30 And brought them out, and said, Sirs,* <u>*what must I do to be saved?*</u>
> *Acts 16:31* <u>*And they said,*</u> <u>**Believe on the Lord Jesus Christ**</u>*, and thou shalt be saved, and thy house.*

We know that the jailer believed because in verse 33 we read that he was baptized in acknowledgment of his belief. But he was not aware of what Scripture elsewhere reveals. He did not know what happened to him internally, or that God chose him before creation. He experienced belief as a personal act (i.e. something he did). But, as is true of all men at the moment of belief, the jailer was unaware of God's "work" of faith in him to bring him to belief. In other words, like all people whom God saves, the jailer was unaware of the true reason for "why" he believed at the moment he was saved. The same is true of Paul, who was an zealous persecutor of Christians. He instantly submitted in obedience to Christ when he was confronted on the road to Damascus. Have you ever asked yourself about "why" Paul resonded so quickly without more questions?

The combination of the command in Acts 16:31, *"**Believe on the Lord Jesus Christ"** and the previously cited verse of John 6:29, which reveals the truth, *"**This is the work of God, that ye believe on him whom he hath sent.**"* provides the perfect illustration of the Augustinian prayer that says to God, "Command what you will, but grant what you command.". God commands Acts 16:31, but He grants this command by the truth of John 6:29.

When we read Paul's statement about "works", in a justification (salvation) context, it disallows any "work of man", including "free will belief".

"*Gal. 2:16 Knowing that a man is not justified by the works of the law*" (even man-created New Testament law.)

To conclude the question of "Belief – whose work is it?", it has been scripturally shown that it is God's work. If all of the prior verses were to disappear, there is yet one passage that unequivocally answers this question. John 1:12-13 is the passage. It will be exposited in Topic 12 below. The granting of salvation apart from any work of man, if true, strikes many as "unfairness" by God and therefore as an unscriptural interpretation. So, in view of this proposed truth of salvation, the question of God's "fairness" needs to be addressed.

Topic 3. God's Fairness

It is popular in Christian theology today, to think that salvation is, and must be, a reward given to men for their "free will" choice to believe. By my count, there are twelve verses in the New Testament which link the preposition "if" to the verb "believe". If you care to check them out, they are: Mar. 9:23; John 3:23, 5:47, 8:24, 11:40, 12:47; Acts 8:37; Rom. 3:3, 4:24, 10:9; 1 Thess. 4:14; and 1 Tim. 2:13. The reason I cite the "if" – "believe" linkage is that they imply a presumption that the act of saving belief is within the willful capability of every person. A person's willful decision to believe the gospel triggers a promised reaction from God. Man's willful decision is clearly required, but the misunderstood truth is the fact that this decision cannot emerge from any "free will". Rom. 10:9 is the best example of an "if" verse because it speaks of salvation in the "if"-"believe" context.

Rom. 10:9 That __if__ thou shalt confess with thy mouth the Lord Jesus, and (if thou) __shalt believe__ *in thine heart that God hath raised him from the dead, __thou shalt be saved__.*

It is logical to presume the necessity of man's free choice in the twelve verses listed above because of the little word "if". The critical error commonly made in theology is the failure to see that man's free will "capability", died in Adam. The fact that these verses do not address is the deeper mystery of "why" or "how", any man believes. The "if" verses about "belief" merely reveal truths about the outcomes of the actions of belief or disbelief. They provide no basis to support the proposition that any choice to believe is "freely" made, apart from the ordained workings of God.

The popular logic that drives the necessity of free will is the principle of "fairness", which is a logical expectation of a "just" God. It is entirely reasonable to expect a "just" God to provide **all** mankind a "fair chance" to believe or reject Him. But, what many Christians fail to acknowledge is the fact that the requirement of the "fair chance" demand, was fully met in the Garden of Eden.

However, because a "just" God can never be convicted for being unjust, (unfair), anywhere, anyhow, and at any time, it necessitates that every person is afforded a "fair chance" in the eyes of the *"judge of all mankind"* (Jesus Christ). A careful search of the Scriptures leads to the inescapable conclusion that Adam's chance had to be the chance of all mankind. In the Garden was the only time that man stood before God in moral innocence. Adam, Eve and all men became corrupt by their choice to sin in Eden.

Two creation principles: "Kinds" and "Moral Inheritance"

There are two principles of creation that deny the possibility that original moral innocence continued on in any of Adam's descendants. The first principle is God's law of "kinds". He has ordained that each "kind" can only produce only like "kinds" and each "kind" is distinct.

> *Gen. 1:24* *And God said,* <u>*Let the earth bring forth the living creature* **after his kind***,* *cattle, and creeping thing, and beast of the earth after his kind: and it was so.*</u>
>
> *1 Cor. 15:39* **All flesh is not the same flesh: but there is one kind of flesh of men, another flesh of beasts, another of fishes, and another of birds.**

By the law of "kinds", the fallen (corrupt) father and mother of all mankind could not possibly have produced a different (uncorrupt) "kind" of offspring.

The second principle of creation, which is the moral subset of the first principle, confirms that corruption cannot produce incorruption. The next four verses document this principle:

1. The moral fate of all men in Adam:

> *1 Cor. 15:21* *For since* **by man came death***, by man came also the resurrection of the dead.*
>
> *1 Cor. 15:22* **For as in Adam all die***, even so in Christ shall all be made alive*

2. the moral state in which they are conceived:

> *Psa. 51:5* *Behold,* <u>***I was shapen in iniquity; and in sin did my mother conceive me***</u>.

135

*1 Cor. 15:42 So also is the resurrection of the dead.
It is __sown in corruption__; it is raised in incorruption:*

3. God's law prohibiting corruption from inheriting incorruption:

Cor. 15:50 Now this I say, brethren, that flesh and blood cannot inherit the kingdom of God; __neither doth corruption inherit incorruption__.

4. the only way that men can escape the state of their death:

1 Pet. 1:23 __Being born again, not of corruptible seed, but of incorruptible, by the word of God__, which liveth and abideth for ever.

Because these creation principles of God cannot be superseded, there is no other scenario in all of creation, other than in the Garden of Eden, where all men could have had the "fair chance" to believe, and where all men once existed in an incorrupt state.

Another truth that provides a irrefutable defense of God's "fairness", is the "without excuse" truth revealed in Romans 1:20.

Rom. 1:20 For __the invisible things of him from the creation of the world are clearly seen__, being understood __by the things that are made__, even his eternal power and Godhead; __so that they are without excuse__:

Adam, Eve and all men in Adam, in the Garden, were, and are, created with an awareness of the "invisible things" of the Godhead and their eternal power. This "awareness" is inherent in every human as creations of God. When the "free will" opportunity of man is properly located in the Bible narrative, and the ensuing fall and incapacitating bondage of man's will is understood, then God's "fairness", in this regard, remains intact. No man can ever claim ignorance of God.

As prophesied, after sinning in the Garden, each man became his own "god". The Bible testifies to the behavior this condition produced in mankind, as they were left to live by their consciences.

> Gen. 6:5 And GOD saw that the wickedness of man was great in the earth, and that **every imagination** of the thoughts of his heart was only **evil continually.**
>
> Jdg. 17:6 In those days there was no king in Israel, but **every man** did that which was right in his own eyes.

Statistically, if "free will" had remained operative in Adam's descendants, then these verses would not have used the words *"every"* in both of these verses. The law of probability says that someone's free will behavior would not have displayed the behavior described in the verses above. Fairness in judgment for evil is mandatory for a God, who is perfectly just. This requirement was met in the provision of man's "fair chance" to obey in the Garden of Eden.

Topic 4. Does God ever command the Impossible of Man?

As noted in the previous topic, the New Testament is full of admonitions "to believe the gospel". It is reasonable to think a man must be able to "freely" do this. God would never command acts of obedience of men, which they are unable to perform, would He? Yes and no. Yes, because God does command acts of obedience that He knows men cannot perform. No, because God has never commanded any act that man does not think he can obey. Here some examples:

To Israel God said:

> *Jos. 1:8 This book of the law shall not depart out of thy mouth; but thou shalt meditate therein day and night, <u>that thou mayest observe</u> **to do according to all that is written therein**: for then thou shalt make thy way prosperous, and then thou shalt have good success.*

Did Israel believe their obedience was possible? Yes. They did not object to God about the demands of the Law. Did Israel ever accomplish "***all that is written therein***"? No. Israel's entire Old Testament history is a cycle of promising to obey – failing to obey – repenting of their failure – re-promising to obey.

To the Pharisees Jesus said:

> *Mat. 22:37 Jesus said unto him, <u>Thou shalt love the Lord thy God</u> **<u>with all</u>** <u>thy heart, and</u> **<u>with all thy</u>** <u>soul, and</u> **<u>with all thy mind.</u>**

Did the Jews ever object to this command? No. Did the Jews, or any man, ever meet these commands as defined by the word "all"? No. Has, or will, any man ever meet them? No.

I disagree with a lot of St. Augustine's Catholic theology, but I repeat the quote that indicated his grasp of God's sovereignty in his commands to men. His famous statement, that ignited a doctrinal firestorm, is still burning. Augustine prayed of God,

> *"Grant what thou commandest and command what thou dost desire."*

By this quote, Augustine first acknowledges that God has the sovereign freedom to command what He wills. But the deeper implication of this historic quote is that because a sovereign God makes commands to fallen, sinful men, He must grant whatsoever He commands of man, because His will is done in all the earth. The Biblical reason underlying such a bold prayer is Augustine's recognition of the duel truth about man's fallen, separated-from-God will, and God's sovereign will that rules His creation including everything that happens therein.

Because of man's sin, the duel truth about man's sin is,

1. Man, in his fallen nature, believes that he is the god of his own life. By nature, man prefers self over obedience to God's commands.
2. Even when any man tries to obey, he is unable to meet God's standards of obedience - perfection.

Topic 5. In Defense of God's work of Election to Salvation

How then, is the Augustinian dilemma solved? Only by God's work of grace in the heart and will of a man, can obedience to the ultimate requirement to believe the gospel for salvation, be met. Many Christians believe that, if God chose those upon whom He would apply His grace that enables saving faith (Eph.1:4), then He unfairly "determined" the fate of everyone by this "choosing" or "not choosing". But, two distinctions need to be understood about who determined what.

1. It is true that all men became sinners "in Adam" (1 Cor. 15:22). But man's sin was "determined" by man alone. It was not determined by God. Adam, Eve and all men in Adam had no compulsion or natural bias to disobey God. God did not make man sin. By the use of their original,

"as created" free will, they chose to yield to the serpent's temptation.

2. What was "determined" by God, before the foundation of the world, was whom He would save from their "self-determined" sin. Critical to the understanding of this point is that the word "before" is a time word. Man sinned in "time", but God made His choices "before time".

God did not make man sin, nor did man's sin determine whom God chose. It is the timing of the two events, God's choosing, and man's sin, that trips up man's theological understanding of the relationship of these events. God specifically tells us about the timing of His choosing in Ephesians 1 – *"before the foundation of the world."* This is a highly controversial passage of Scripture.

If it was true that before time began, God chose some people to receive salvation and not others, it means that God was showing "respect of persons". The truth that God is *"no respecter of persons"* was made in Chapter 6 above, regarding Abraham. Nevertheless, many Christians assert that the doctrine of election to salvation, if true, would be a showing of "respect of persons" by God. Therefore, they conclude election is a false doctrine. Since the concept of God's election cannot be erased from Scripture, opponents strive to connect God's elective act towards some other purpose. Ephesians, chapter 1 is where the topic of election (God's sovereign choosing) is discussed.

> *Eph. 1:4 According **as he hath chosen us** in him before the foundation of the world, **that we should be holy** and **without blame before him** in love:*
> *Eph. 1:5 Having predestinated us unto **the adoption of children by Jesus Christ to himself**, according to the good pleasure of his will,*

> *Eph. 1:6 To* **the praise of the glory of his grace,** *wherein he hath made us accepted in the beloved.*
> *Eph. 1:7 In whom we have redemption through his blood,* **the forgiveness of sins,** *according to the riches of his grace;*
> *Eph. 1:8 Wherein he hath* **abounded toward us in all wisdom and prudence;**
> *Eph 1:9 Having* **made known unto us the mystery of his will,** *according to his good pleasure which he hath purposed in himself:*
> *Eph 1:10 That in the dispensation of the fulness of times he might* **gather together in one all things in Christ,** *both which are in heaven, and which are on earth; even in him:*
> *Eph 1:11 In whom also we have* **obtained an inheritance,** *being predestinated according to the purpose of him who worketh all things after the counsel of his own will:*

This section of Ephesians 1 presents a real obstacle to "free will" doctrine. A common spin offered is that the "choosing" of verse 4 refers only to being chosen to be *"holy and without blame before him"*. Any attempt by free will (Arminian) doctrine to try to deflect the fact that verses 4 through 14 of Ephesians Chapter 1 are enumerating the deep truths about God's sovereign work of election to salvation, is theologically irrational. Read the list of descriptive "expressions" (in bold type) that appear in the passage of verses 4 to 11:

v. 4 ....*we should be* **holy** *and* **without blame** *before him in love:*

v. 5 ....*Having* **predestinated us** *unto the* **adoption of children by Jesus Christ** *to himself....*

v. 6 ....*wherein he hath made us* **accepted in the beloved.**

v. 7 *In whom we* **have redemption** *through his blood, the for-giveness of sins....*

v. 11 *...we* **have obtained an inheritance, being predestinated** *according to the purpose of him who worketh all things* **after the counsel of his own will:**

A common defense against the doctrine of election is the argument that the word "salvation" does not appear in any of the verses above. The word salvation does not appear in John 14:6 either, but everyone knows what the topic is.

> *John 14:6 Jesus saith unto him, I am the way, the truth, and the life: no man cometh unto the Father, but by me.*

The argument, to defend free will by trying to disconnect all of the above "expressions" (in bold type), from the gift of salva-tion, is doctrinal desperation. To be "predestinated" to any of these blessings, a person must be saved and thus predestined to salvation by default. The interpretive logic that separates predestination from salvation is as futile as a hypothetical that would contend that man was predestined to "breathe air", but not to being born. You cannot be predestined to any of the bold type phrases above and not be predestined to salvation. It is im-possible to be *"holy and without blame before him"* unless you have been saved. If one was predestined to be *"holy and without blame before him"*, then he or she was predestined to salvation.

That false interpretation aside, God's elective work was done before anyone existed so there could be no accusations of *"respect of persons"* by God, because, before the foundation of the world, no one possessed any virtue that could merit their salvation.

The following passages in Romans also demonstrate the sovereign prerogative of God's will, as well as a defense of any charge against His elective choosing of God showing "*respect*" to those He chooses.

> *Rom. 9:11 (***For the children being not yet born,*** neither having done any good or evil, that the purpose of God according to election might stand, not of works, but of him that calleth;)*

> *Rom. 9:13 As it is written, <u>Jacob have I loved, but Esau have I hated</u>.*

(Note "when" this choice was made.)

> *Rom. 9:14 What shall we say then? Is there unrighteousness with God? God forbid.*

(If, from verse 13, anyone would charge God with unrighteousness by showing "respect" for Jacob by loving him and not Esau, the answer is "God forbid".)

> *Rom. 9:15 For he saith to Moses, I will have mercy on whom I will have mercy, and I will have compassion on whom I will have compassion.*

(This verse is the answer that explains the "God forbid" response in verse 14. In verse 15, God is confirming the truth of Dan. 4:35 where it says that "*....he doeth according to his will in the army of heaven, and among the inhabitants of the earth:...*" His will is done in heaven and on earth.) Another verse against "free will" is:

> *Rom. 9:16 So then <u>it is not of him that willeth</u>, <u>nor of him that runneth</u>, but of God that sheweth mercy.*

The inescapable conclusion is the truth that being "loved", i.e. "chosen", i.e. "saved" is not reliant or dependent upon man's "will" or "running" [effort or work]. It is by the will of God alone that all mercy is shown.

The correct context of verses 4 to 11 of Ephesians 1 reveals the depth of the blessings that the recipients of this glorious gift of salvation are predestined to receive. One cannot receive these predestined blessings without also being predestined to salvation. This passage in Ephesians prompts great consternation in free will expositors.

Another well known verse that Arminian doctrine twists to warp the doctrine of predestination to salvation is drawn from Romans chapter 8. Paul writes,

> *Rom. 8:29* ***For whom he did foreknow, he also did predestinate*** *to be conformed to the image of his Son, that he might be the firstborn among many brethren.*

Arminian (free will) doctrine is especially fond of interpreting this verse as a reference to the omniscient foreknowledge of God about who would believe. In "free will" doctrine, His "foreknowledge" of which people will believe becomes the "cause" of His election (choice) of any person. They reason that, because God is omniscient, He foreknew which men would believe the gospel. There are four problems with this interpretation.

First, while it is true that God foreknows everything that man will do, including the first act of sin in the Garden, God also knows everything that man can't do as a consequence of that sin. Repetition being one of the best tools for learning, I must repeat 1 Corinthians 4: 12 as a specific revelation of what natural (sinful) man cannot do.

> *1 Cor. 2:14 But the* **natural man receiveth not** *the things of the Spirit of God: for they are foolishness unto him:* **neither** **can** *he know them, because they are spiritually discerned.*

Second, applying another point of repetition, while God sovereignly determined those whose wills He would quicken (Eph. 2:1) to believe, He did not determine, or compel, their sin that spiritually disabled their wills. It must be noted that Romans 8:29 speaks specifically about "**whom** *he did foreknow*", rather than speaking of His knowledge about "what they would do". The emphasis here is on the *"whom"*, not the "what", of God's foreknowledge. If God's predestining of select people was dependent upon the actions of their free wills, this verse would be the place to have stated it.

A third problem is created by the mechanics or rationale, behind a "free will" choice. As was previously mentioned, the making of a "free will" choice presumes the possession of a certain level of perception and information on the part of the individual. In theological circles, this level is, at times, defined as the individual reaching an age of accountability. Infants and young children cannot be expected to make decisions on this level. Apart from the problem posed by this segment of mankind, it often takes years for many adults to come to belief. If God's predestinating is dependent upon "what" men will do regarding belief or unbelief, how can time and the ages ever end? Within all living humanity, there will always be some who are in the process of making this crucial "free will" choice. However, Scripture says that this world will come to an end. This would mean that the "decision clock" is going to run out on some people before they reach the age of accountability or have their moment of perspicacity (mental enlightenment) in adulthood. Because of the promised end of the world, some people would miss their opportunity in their lifetime, to discern, to choose, and thus, merit

God's choosing of them because of their choice. How could this ever be fair? The end of the world will not leave any of God's elect unsaved.

The fourth problem, that will be discussed in depth in Topic 13, is that the "free will" view is a blatant contradiction to John 1:13, which specifically excludes man's will from any causative role in his salvation. Of three possible causes of salvation: man's will alone, a combination of co-operation of man's will and God's will, or God's will alone; there can be only one cause of salvation. John 1:13 gives us the answer.

The previous verses, arguments, and Augustine's quote about the necessity of God granting what He commands of men, reveal the only reason behind anyone's saving faith – by God's grace and will alone.

Topic 6. The Scriptural Components of the Salvation Sequence

So, if all salvations depend on God and He is not a "respector of persons", how does He sovereignly accomplish the act of "saving faith" that He commands, among all of His elect? In a nutshell, the verses below outline the components of the "*work of God*", which result in the generation of saving faith in a man. This "work" consists of a five-step sequence, all of which are the exclusive domain of God.

1. Eph. 1:4 - God's pre-creation choosing of whom He will save; (A secret known only to God.)
2. Acts 16:14 - God's opening of a person's heart to effectual hearing; (If God did this for Lydia, then it must be true for all salvations. Otherwise, God "respected" Lydia.)
3. Rom. 10:17 - the hearing **by** the word of God (a spiritual, not merely physical, hearing in an "opened" heart);
4. Eph. 2:8 - the gift of faith given, by God's grace, to those who heard the word of God with an "opened" heart:

5. Rom. 10:9 – the resulting saving faith and confession produced by the very gift of faith received.

Someone might object that the step of belief is still dependent upon the willful response of the individual and therefore, each man has some responsibility in the salvation process. This assertion would be as illogical as giving an infant, just emerged from the womb, credit for his life by the act of breathing.

If it is helpful, consider these steps in reverse order:

step 5 is the result of step 4

step 4 is the result of step 3

step 3 accompanies step 2*

(*steps 2 & 3 are virtually simultaneous)

(steps 2 & 3 combined equal "effectual hearing")

step 2 depends on step 1*

(* step 1, God's act of election is a "fait accompli" by God. It is an act that is divinely ordained, divinely completed, irreversible, and inevitable in its fulfillment.)

The logic of these Scriptural facts dictates that because of Step 1, Steps 2,3,4, & 5 are assured.

The following chart is a visual effort to display the connectivity of the Scriptural evidence of how the pre-creation salvation "decrees" of God are granted by the sovereign "workings" of God, upon "whom He wills it", at the specific time "He wills it":

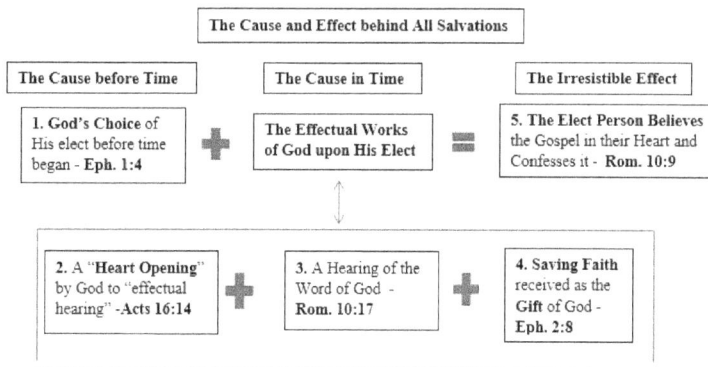

The Cause and Effect behind All Salvations

The Cause before Time	The Cause in Time	The Irresistible Effect
1. God's Choice of His elect before time began - Eph. 1:4	The Effectual Works of God upon His Elect	5. The Elect Person Believes the Gospel in their Heart and Confesses it - Rom. 10:9
2. A "Heart Opening" by God to "effectual hearing" -Acts 16:14	3. A Hearing of the Word of God - Rom. 10:17	4. Saving Faith received as the Gift of God - Eph. 2:8

The will of man participates in step 5 (the effect), but not by any "freedom" of man's will. Instead, it happens because, by the will of God the "enslaved" will of the elect person was "freed" (enabled) to believe. These essential pre-salvation workings of God are addressed in depth in my book titled, *"99% Grace?" "How Free is Man's Will?".*

What is it that the recipients of this sequential "work of God" are to believe in step 5? It is "the gospel". The essence of the gospel, which remains as God's present requirement for men to believe is, salvation by "faith alone". The clearest proclamation of it is found in 1 Cor. 15:1-4. But, the very simplicity of the "by faith alone" requirement, makes it an easy target for Satan to use to persuade men, through their pride, that their salvation is, in some manner, dependent upon their willing co-operation. Why? Because men see this as a requirement which they can, and must, obey by their own wills. What Satan accomplishes by this deception is a doctrinal blindness in men to the Biblical truth about their own spiritual deadness. It is a spiritual deadness so deep, that any possibility of man's self-escape from his bondage in sin is denied. The verses describing this deadness will be shown and discussed in Topic 8.

The common view of many Christians is that it is each person's responsibility to "hear", "process" and "understand" the gospel call. By their own intellect or perceptiveness, they can make their personal decision to believe or reject the gospel, apart from any compulsion or influence of God. The personal belief decision, made in this manner, becomes the first step (the cause) of their salvation, which thereby precipitates God's predestinating choice of them.

While it is a Scriptural fact that men's wills are involved in the salvation decision, the reason for the involvement of their wills is misunderstood.

Topic 7. God's Irresistible Grace of Drawing

People who insist on their "free will" participation in salvation must concede that both God and the Son must have an essential role in man's salvation. These truths are confirmed in the gospel of John. John documents the dual roles of God, the Father and Christ, the Son in the "coming" of any person to God (salvation), These indispensable truths are defined in the verses below.

> *John 6:44* ***No man can come to me, except the Father which hath sent me draw him****: and I will raise him up at the last day.*
> *John 6:65 And he said, Therefore said I unto you,* ***that no man can come unto me, except it were given unto him of my Father.***
> *John 14:6 Jesus saith unto him, I am the way, the truth, and the life:* ***no man cometh unto the Father, but by me.***

The contention that salvation relies solely upon the person's willingness to accept or reject the gospel, regardless of whatever influencing work God has exerted upon them, implies that any "drawing" work by the Father, or by the Son, are not irresistible. The insinuation that God's drawing work can fail, creates some serious implications. By this theological position, it is conceding the possibility that people such as Abraham, Mary the mother of Jesus, the twelve disciples, or the apostle Paul (just to name a few), could all have refused the call of God by the exercise of their respective "free wills". By this view, the obedient responses recorded in Scripture, by each of the fore-mentioned persons, were "free will" acts. By this logic, the course of Scripture could have been drastically altered. The ultimate implication of this theology must conclude that the path of all of the human histories that has transpired, both before and after the Garden of Eden, ultimately rests upon the will of man, not God.

If this was true, here are some possibilities of how Scripture could have been changed:

Abram could have responded differently in Genesis 12. After hearing the LORD's call and promises to him, Abram's response is recorded in verse 4. Scripture says:

> *Gen. 12:4* ***So Abram departed, as the LORD had spoken unto him;*** *and Lot went with him: and Abram was seventy and five years old when he departed out of Haran.*

But, if his will was truly "free" in the Arminian sense, verse 4 could have read:

> *Gen. 12:4 So Abram **refused to obey**, as the LORD had spoken unto him; and Lot **stayed** with him: and Abram was seventy and five years old when he **remained in** Haran.*

Mary's response to the angel Gabriel in Luke 1:38 could have been as shown in this bold type modified verse:

> *Luke 1:38 And Mary said, Behold the handmaid of the Lord; be it **not** unto me according to thy word. And the angel departed from her.*

The angel would have had to move on to another virgin.

The names of the twelve disciples could have been different, if their decision to follow Jesus was left entirely to the discretion of personal wills.

The apostle Paul in Acts 9:6, instead of answering Jesus by saying, "*Lord, what wilt thou have me to do?*", could have replied,

"I don't believe what you say, so I am continuing on my mission to Damascus."

There is a common response that Arminians (free will proponents) will offer in explanation of their position. They argue that salvation is a "gift", prepared by, and presented by, God to men for their belief in the gospel. "Gift logic," says that it is each person's individual responsibility to "accept or reject" a gift. This is normal behavior in response to the offer of a gift. This logic is true, in a human context, but the possibility of any "free will" rejection of the gift of salvation, ignores, not only the three *"coming"* verses, quoted above from John's gospel, but also another crucial statement by Jesus recorded in John's gospel. Read the statement by Jesus about those who were given to Him (Jesus) by the Father.

> *John 6:39 And this is the Father's will which hath sent me, that of **all which he hath given me I should lose nothing,** but should raise it up again at the last day.*

A pertinent question one should ask after reading John 6:39 is, "When did the "giving" of John 6:39 occur?" Scripture provides the answer.

> *2 Thess. 2:13 But we are bound to give thanks alway to God for you, brethren beloved of the Lord, because **God hath from the beginning chosen you to salvation** through sanctification of the Spirit and belief of the truth:*

(Predestination critics can't escape the phrase *"chosen you to salvation",* in this verse.)

Let me summarize the crucial points of these four important verses cited above.

We learn from:

John 14:6 "....*no man cometh unto the Father, but by me.*" Jesus is the only way to come to God.

John 6:44 "....*No man can come to me, except the Father which hath sent me draw him.*" God must draw all who come. and from:

John 6:39 "....*all which he hath given me I should lose nothing,*" None of those who, are drawn by God, and come through Jesus, will be lost.

and finally....2 Thess. 2:13 "*.God hath from the beginning chosen you to salvation....*" The "giving", of all who are drawn and will never be lost, is assured because they were God's choice made from the beginning. (More specifically, made from "*before the foundation of the world*" - Eph. 1:4)

Regarding the "*coming*" of any person under the parameters of John 14:6 and John 6:44, it must be asked, "What is the process by which the chosen ones will come?" Jesus revealed "part" of the answer regarding the "*coming*" process in John 6.

> *John 6:45 It is written in the prophets, And they shall be all* (the "all" who "come" in verse 44 above) *taught of God. **Every man therefore that hath heard, and hath learned of the Father, cometh unto me.***

If John 6:45 was the complete answer, then the act of "coming to Christ" would be totally dependent upon a person's ability to perceive (hear) (*hath heard*) and their intelligence (*hath learned*). As just laid out in Topic 8 above, there is, thankfully, there is more to the answer of the question "how does belief happen?" than is stated in John 6:45, because it is an indisputable fact, that men are not equally blessed with the abilities of perception and intelligence. If salvation was dependent upon an individual's abilities to learn and understand, then it would mean that, God would have to be a *"respector of persons"* in the *"coming"* of any-one to Christ, because men are not equally endowed with these abilities, He would be respecting "those who get it". But the Bible is explicit. God is not a "respecter of persons" (Acts 10:34).

Man's willingness to *"come"* must go beyond his perception and intelligence. Why? Because all of Adam's descendants have a "nature problem". The ultimate limiting factor of "willingness" is fallen man's nature. If man's nature, in his descent from Adam, remained as free and unbiased as the nature in which God cre-ated Adam, then every person would surely be able to, and re-sponsible to, make their own, personal choice about God's offer of salvation in Christ. But the Bible provides no support to the proposal that the nature of Adam's descendants continued in the same of innocence as that of Adam's created nature.

Topic 8. Why Spiritually "dead" Men cannot "come"

Apart from the over-arching truth of God's predestinating choice of whom He will draw to salvation and whom He will leave in the grip of their own sin (Eph. 1:4; Rom. 9:15), the de-lusion (lie) that fallen (lost) men still have the ability and the responsibility to choose to believe is one of Satan's most subtle and successful deceptions. Scripture describes those who are saved (quickened), as previously being, *"dead in their sins and trespasses. "*

> *Eph. 2:1 And **you hath he quickened**, who were **dead in trespasses and sins**;*

This pre-salvation condition, without doubt, applies to all men.

> *Rom. 3:10 As it is written, <u>There is none righteous</u>, no, not one:*

> *Rom. 3:11* <u>*There is none that understandeth, there*</u>
> <u>*is none that seeketh*</u> *after God.*
> *Rom. 3:12* <u>*They are all gone out of the way, they are*</u>
> <u>*together become unprofitable;*</u> **there is none that**
> **doeth good, no, not one.**

The words "none" and "all" that are used in this Romans 3 passage are all-inclusive words that encompass all mankind. David further confirms that the state of man's sin (and resultant fallen state) did not simply "evolve" during their lifetimes. Every descendant of Adam was conceived in it.

> *Psa. 51:5 Behold,* **I was shapen in iniquity; and in**
> **sin did my mother conceive me.**

This was not self-deprecating speculation by David, nor is it a casting of the blame for his sin upon his mother. It could only have come to him by a revelation from God. Thus, if it was true about his conception, it is true of all men. We are all born "dead" (spiritually); not "ill", but "dead".

The error of the view about man's free will ability to "believe" the gospel and "come" to God is a consequence of the failure to grasp the Scriptural truths about the degree of man's depravity (spiritual separation from God). The letters of the apostle Paul offer a variety of references to the dire spiritual state of fallen mankind. The following are just a few examples of the descriptive language that Paul used in verses that define man's relationship with God:

> *Rom. 5:10 For if,* **when we were enemies,** *we were*
> *reconciled to God by the death of his Son,much*
> *more, being reconciled, we shall be saved by his life.*
> *Rom. 7:6 But now* <u>*we are delivered from the law,*</u>
> <u>*that* **being dead wherein we were held**</u>*; that we*

*should serve in newness of spirit, and not in the old-
ness of the letter.*

Gal. 4:3 Even so we, <u>when we were children, were</u> **<u>in
bondage under the elements of the world</u>**:

Eph. 2:1 And you hath he quickened, **who were <u>dead
in trespasses and sins;</u>**

Col. 1:21 And <u>you, that were sometime</u> **<u>alienated
and enemies in your mind by wicked works</u>**, *yet
now hath he reconciled.*

Col. 2:13 And **<u>you, being dead in your sins</u>** *and the
uncircumcision of your flesh, hath he quickened together with him, having forgiven you all trespasses;*

These descriptive phrases, highlighted in bold type, eliminate
any possibility that the degree of man's sin problem is a casual
one. These verses present a problem for the premise of man's ac-
cepting salvation by his free will as the solution to his condemnation under sin. The bondage in sin is absolute. 2 Cor. 5:14 un-
ambiguously defines the extent of the reason for Christ's death:

*2 Cor. 5:14 For the love of Christ constraineth us;
because we thus judge, that* **<u>if one died for all, then
were all dead:</u>**

Men cannot "resurrect" themselves from the dead, physically
or spiritually.

Topic 9. All men "in Adam"

1 Cor. 15:22 For as **<u>in Adam all die</u>**, *even so in
Christ shall all be made alive.*

The implied truth, that must be logically drawn from the truth *"...in Adam all die,"*, is that "all were alive". Alive where? In the same "one" in which "all were dead" – Adam. Verses like Eph. 2:1 and Col. 2:13 above, define the context of the *"all dead"* – *"dead in sins"*. The failure of "free will" theology is its' inability to Scripturally explain, how "dead" men, by their own powers, can understand the gospel offer and their need for salvation. They must construct a milder context for their definition of "dead". The context of death in these verses is spiritual. When something is dead, whether spiritual or physical, the recipient of either death can do nothing by their own power to overcome or escape the condition. As previously noted, 1 Corinthians 2:14 confirms the fact that "spiritually dead" (natural) men "cannot" perceive spiritual things. This verse disallows any presumed power or ability of man's free will to independently perceive his helplessness and choose to escape his state of spiritual death by belief.

The paradox of God condemning men for something that they "unable" to do was previously discussed in Topic 4. A just God could not send a person to hell without providing the opportunity to exercise a willful choice to obey or disobey Him. This would violate the attribute of God's justice because He is just.

> *Isa. 45:21 ....there is no God else beside me; **a just God** and a Saviour; there is none beside me.*
> *Rev. 15:3 ....marvellous are thy works, Lord God Almighty; **just and true are thy ways,** ....*

Because God is perfectly just, the question becomes, "Where in the history of creation did all men have a fair opportunity to be responsible?" The only Biblical, and irrefutable, answer has to be "in Adam".

Original Sin

The doctrine which expresses the truth that shows all mankind as a participant in Adam's sin is called the doctrine of original sin. This doctrine causes great distress to many Christians. Nevertheless, it provides the only possible satisfaction to the theological need for every man to have a "fair chance" to obey or disobey God. The issue of God's fairness was discussed at the beginning of Part 2. If man's "free will" chance to obey did not happen "in Adam", then those who reject the "Original Sin" doctrine must conceive some other Biblically irrefutable explanation for how, or when, all men receive their "fair chance" to exercise their free and unbiased will to believe the gospel. Below is the definition of this doctrine as found in Wikipedia. Note the last two sentences of the unbiased Wikipedia definition, which explain the wide range of views of the doctrine of "Original Sin" held by men.

> ***Original sin***, *also called* <u>ancestral sin</u>,[1] *is a* <u>*Christian*</u> belief in the state of sin in which *humanity has existed since the* <u>fall of man</u>, *stemming from* <u>Adam and Eve</u>*'s rebellion in* <u>Eden</u>, *namely the sin of disobedience in consuming the* <u>forbidden fruit</u> *from the* tree of the knowledge of good and evil This condition has been characterized in many ways, *ranging from something as insignificant as* <u>*a slight deficiency, or a tendency toward sin*</u> *yet without collective guilt, referred to as a "sin nature", to something as drastic as* <u>total depravity</u> *or* <u>automatic guilt of all humans through</u> <u>*collective guilt*</u>.[3]

The range between the extremes of the "characterizations" of this doctrine is significant. It represents the gap between the two theological poles, which epitomize the two opposing views of how God redeems men to salvation. Although some theologies completely isolate Adam's sin as only impacting him, many "free will" advocates, rather than blatantly rejecting the doctrine of original sin, subscribe to the definition which declares that mankind merely inherited *a slight deficiency or a tendency toward sin*. This view permits man the ability to self-correct from his *"tendency toward sin"* by his free will capacity to choose to believe the gospel.

In a sense, this view reduces the decision to believe the gospel to the level of a personal decision, similar to a decision to quit smoking. By use of the personal faculty of reason and will, some men conclude that smoking is bad for them and give it up. Likewise, after consideration of what Scripture says, some men make a mental decision to believe that the gospel is the best way to salvation. By this decision, they believe that any consequence from the *"tendency toward sin"* is overcome.

The position of this author stands in complete agreement with the last Wikipedia characterization of this doctrine, which defines the "original sin" condition of all men as being in *total depravity or automatic guilt of all humans through collective guilt*." In a nutshell, mankind has a spiritually fatal sin problem. Scripture is unequivocal about it.

> *Rom. 3:10 As it is written, **There is none righteous**, no, not one:*

And

> *Rom. 3:23 For **all have sinned**, and come short of the glory of God;*

This characterization is the only possible, Biblically correct, view. The Biblical fact of men deemed as *"dead in sins"* (Eph. 2:1; Col. 2:13) cannot be spun or twisted into an interpretation that views mankind as acquiring just a *"slight deficiency"* or merely having "a *tendency toward sin*". If this were true, the doctrine should be called "original deficiency", not "original sin". Read again how the Bible explicitly defines the "in Adam" location of all men. Note how these verses indisputably link connect all men to Adam.

> *1 Cor. 15:22 For as* **in Adam all die**, *even so in Christ shall all be made alive.*
> *Rom. 5:12 Wherefore,* <u>*as* **by one man** *sin entered into the world, and death by sin; and so death passed upon all men, for that all have sinned:*</u>

The "in the loins" truth

Many dispute the context of all men being "in Adam" as a biological fact. To this objection, I appeal to the revelation in the book of Hebrews about Levi, from whom the priests of Israel originated. The author of Hebrews, who I strongly believe was Paul, wrote the following verses regarding Levi, Abraham and the mysterious priest Melchisedec. Remembering that all Scripture is written under the inspiration of the Holy Spirit. Paul is not just offering mere conjecture when he wrote the following:

> *Heb. 7:9 And as I may so say,* **Levi also, who receiveth tithes, payed tithes in Abraham.**
> *Heb. 7:10 For* **he was yet in the loins of his father** (Abraham), <u>*when Melchisedec met him.*</u>

Here in Scripture, it was affirmed that Levi, who was a third-generation descendant of Abraham, was, *"yet in the loins of his father when Melcisedec met him."* If it is true that Levi was *"was in the loins"* of his great grandfather, Abraham, then it is equally true that all men, who descended from Adam, were also *"in the loins"* of Adam. All men are determined as being *"in Adam"* not only in both a seminal context, but also in a judicial context by the one who is *"the judge of all the earth"*(Gen. 18:25).

To demonstrate the proposition that all died *"in Adam"*, consider the two syllogisms, offered below, to prove that all men not only died *"in Adam"*, but logically, also lived, and therefore, sinned *"in Adam"*.

1. For anything to die, it must first be alive. *In Adam all die.* (1 Cor. 15:22) Therefore, *"in Adam"*, all were alive.
2. The penalty for sin is death *(Eze 18:20) The soul that sinneth, it shall die. (Eze 18:20) In Adam all die.* (1 Cor. 15:22) Therefore, *"death passed upon all men"* because *"by* (in) *one man"* (Adam), *"all have sinned."* (Rom. 5:12)

Critics may object to the logic of these two syllogisms, but they are fighting against the biblical truth of all men being *"in Adam"*. A just God, who is *"the judge of all the earth"* (Gen. 18:25), cannot judge men as justifiably guilty of rejecting Him, unless they were "freely" able to choose to reject Him. God would be unjust to "slay" any man who lacked a "free choice" opportunity.

> *Gen. 18:25 That be far from thee to do after this manner, to slay the righteous with the wicked: and that the righteous should be as the wicked, that be far from thee:* **Shall not the Judge of all the earth do right?**

To satisfy the logic and demand of justice, it can only be *"in Adam"*, and *"in Adam all"*, that all men had the prerequisite "free will" opportunity to choose obedience or disobedience. Thus, by their "free" choice, "in Adam", all men deserve the judgment of death for sin. This fact explains the all-important doctrinal truth of all men being justly judged guilty. It is because they were all *"in Adam".*

Topic 10. Free Will lived "in Adam" and It died "in Adam"

Before further examination of the "in Adam" concept, allow me to digress and make a grammatical adjustment to the expression "free will", that has been used up to this point in this book. Although I have advanced the concept of God's application of the "fixed gulf" mechanisms as a means to block fallen man's "free will" efforts to "save" himself, I need to modify the expression "free will" with the more theologically correct expression. The accurate definition of the will, since the Garden of Eden, would be man's "presumed free will". "Free-will" is the term for what many people think they employ in their normal decision-making processes. Just because mankind cannot see or feel the bondage that governs their will, does not change the fact of it.

The truth about the will of every man is that, since the sin in the Garden, man's will has never been "free", despite their belief and their perceived experience to the contrary. There was a point in the history of mankind when they turned from the righteous commands of God. This turning moment is captured by Paul as he wrote in Romans 1. Read these verses along with my inserted, bold type question, that ought to be asked and answered.

Rom. 1:18 For the wrath of God is revealed from heaven against all ungodliness and unrighteousness of men, (all men, 1 Cor. 15:22) *who hold the truth in unrighteousness;* **(when was this?)** *Rom. 1:19 Because that which may be known of God is manifest in them;* (all men) *for God hath shewed it unto them.* **(when was this?)** *Rom. 1:20 For the invisible things of him from the creation of the world are clearly seen, being understood by the things that are made, even his eternal power and Godhead;* **(when was this?)** *so that they are without excuse:*

Rom. 1:21 Because that, when they knew God, they glorified him not as God, neither were thankful; but became vain in their imaginations, and their foolish heart was darkened. **(when was this?)** *Rom 1:22 Professing themselves to be wise, they became fools,* **(when was this?)**

Verse 21 specifically describes the "turning moment". It evokes the pertinent question of **"when"** did this happen. If your answer to the question of **"when was this?"** is at any time other than "in the Garden" and "in Adam", then you must Biblically explain when, and how, the reign of sin universally happened to all mankind, if not in Eden. For those who contend that the "turning moment" is a moment that occurs in every individual's life after their conception, they have to explain why infants and children die, given the Biblical truth that the only reason for death is sin. Infants and young children cannot grasp the concept of sin and therefore, cannot possibly be capable of, or accountable for, having *"vain imaginations"* or *"darkened hearts"*. But Paul goes on to write that *"...sin hath reigned unto death"*. It did not just "reign" over accountable people. Death's reign reaches into the womb.

> *Psa 51:5 Behold, I was shapen in iniquity; and in sin did my mother conceive me.*

> *Rom. 5:21 That as sin hath reigned unto death,* **(when?)** *even so might grace reign through righteousness unto eternal life by Jesus Christ our Lord.* **(by His death, burial, and resurrection)**

Ever since mankind's fall into sin, in the Garden of Eden, the will of every man has been in bondage to the higher power of Satan. Paul reminds the believers in Ephesus of this bondage prior to their salvation.

> *Eph. 2:2 Wherein __in time past ye walked according__*
> *__to the course of this world, according to the prince__*
> *__of the power of the air__, the spirit that now worketh*
> *in the children of disobedience:*
> *Eph. 2:3 Among whom also we all had our conversa-*
> *tion in times past in the lusts of our flesh, fulfilling*
> *the desires of the flesh and of the mind; and __were by__*
> *__nature the children of wrath__, even __as others.__*

All believers have been delivered from the bondage of this nature. The nature as *"children of wrath",* is where all of the *"others"* of verse 3 will remain, unless, by God's grace, they are His elect and, as such, will be saved in the future. While the concept of men doing what was *"right in their own eyes"* is a scripturally documented condition (Judges 17:6 and 21:25), they are, in reality, acting in accord to their nature, as plainly defined in Eph. 2:3 above. Men would act in accord with the prophecy of Satan in Genesis 3:5 by becoming the arbiters of right and wrong.

> *Gen. 3:5 For God doth know that in the day ye eat*
> *thereof, __then your eyes shall be opened, and ye__*
> *__shall be as gods, knowing good and evil.__*

Two Masters

There is a teaching of Jesus in the Bible that indirectly implies the fact that the wills of all created human beings are subject to some higher power. Within the lengthy Sermon on the Mount, Jesus made a point, which is very relevant to this discussion. Jesus taught:

> *Mat. 6:24 __No man can serve two masters__: for ei-*
> *ther he will hate the one, and love the other; or else*

*he will hold to the one, and despise the other. <u>Ye can-
not serve God and mammon</u>.*

What is not directly said here, but is nevertheless true, is the fact that every human being serves some master in a moral context. No human is "master-free". No human is a true free agent. No man is really "his own god", even though the effect of eating of "the tree of the knowledge of good and evil" left men in the belief that they are "gods" of their own lives. Men, being lower than God and lower than angels (including Satan), will serve either God or Satan. In another teaching on the Mount of Olives, Jesus stated this principle about sin's dominion over people.

> *John 8:34 Jesus answered them, Verily, verily, I say
> unto you, <u>__Whosoever committeth sin is the ser-
> vant of sin.__</u>*

(The point was previously made that "all men" sinned "in Adam".) Paul confirmed the "servanthood" principle in Romans.

> *Rom. 6:16   Know ye not, that <u>__to whom ye yield
> yourselves servants to obey, his servants ye are__</u> to
> whom ye obey; whether of sin unto death, or of obe-
> dience unto righteousness?*
> *Rom. 6:17   But God be thanked, that <u>__ye were the
> servants of sin__</u>, but ye have obeyed from the heart
> that form of doctrine which was delivered you.*

The word "servants" in the KJV comes from the Greek word "doulas" which literally means "slave". It is interesting that Strong's Greek Dictionary defines this word "servant" as "*a slave,(literally or figuratively, either involuntarily or voluntarily.)*". All of these adjectives apply to the "servant" status under discussion in verses 16 and 17 above. The "*servants of sin*" condition was unknowingly, yet voluntarily, chosen by Adam (all mankind) in the garden of Eden. It is now a "servanthood" that is both literal and figurative. It is a "servanthood" which now is beyond the reach of any voluntary escape by the power of any "presumed" free will of man. It is a "servanthood" that was voluntarily chosen, but not voluntarily escapable.

Scripture does not leave anyone beyond the effect of the "reign" of sin.

> Rom. 3:23 For **all have sinned**, and come short of the glory of God;

When man sinned in the Garden, guess whose servant he became?

In this life, even those saved by faith in the gospel are still subject to the effects of this "servanthood". In Romans chapter 7, there is an interesting commentary by Paul about his struggle with a "duel servanthood". In this chapter, Paul writes about two powers (masters) to which he is still subject. While he confesses to the reality of these two powers (masters), Paul confirms the fact that his flesh is still in bondage to one master while, in his mind, as a believer, he now desires to serve another. His confession is the dilemma of all believers – he is subject to both powers, but cannot simultaneously serve both powers. The result is an internal spiritual war.

> Rom. 7:18 For I know that in me (that is, in my flesh,) dwelleth no good thing: <u>for to **will** is present with me; but how to perform that which is good I find not</u>.
> Rom. 7:21 I find then a law, that, <u>when I would do good, evil is present with me</u>.
> Rom.7:22 For <u>I delight in the law of God after the inward man</u>:

*Rom. 7:23 But **I see another law in my members, warring against the law of my mind, and bringing me into captivity to the law of sin which is in my members**.*

In Ephesians, Paul described the powers of evil that are man's real enemy.

*Eph. 6:12 For **we wrestle** not against flesh and blood, but **against principalities, against powers, against the rulers of the darkness of this world, against spiritual wickedness in high places.***

In Scripture, there is no third option provided, of serving only "self". God has allowed Satan to enslave men with the illusion that they can go through life doing what *"seemeth right in their own eyes"*. But, the illusion of serving "self" is, in reality, serving only one of the two possible masters. In Romans 7, Paul's eyes were opened to this spiritual truth. It is a significant piece of some "eye-opening" information that Satan did not reveal to mankind in the Garden, nor to any of mankind since Eden.

Man as "a god"

Satan is not incapable of telling men "partial truth". Partial truth is what Satan, in Genesis 3:5, told Adam and Eve. It was true that they would experience feeling as if they were their "own gods". What Satan omitted to reveal to them was their new state of moral and mental servitude to him as their new master. All men would, from that day forward, naively think that they are their "own gods".

> *Gen. 3:5 For God doth know that in the day ye eat thereof, then <u>your eyes shall be opened, and **ye shall be as gods**, knowing good and evil.</u>*

The result of this effective deception has been the on-going, natural perception by men in the belief that they have a totally "free will". Under the bondage of this deception, Satan will successfully lead all of the non-elect mass of humanity to their eternal doom in Hell. He captured them in Eden and will keep them captive into their final judgment to Hell. Only those who are the "elect of God" (Eph. 1-4, 2 Thess. 2:13) will be sovereignly delivered from their bondage to this deception. All of those who remain in Satan's deception will be content to live as "gods" over their own lives and their own destinies. Only the grace of God can free any person from the delusion of being their own "god".

Two Spiritual States

Consider this irony. So many Christians, without question, gladly accept their salvation by the means of the atoning work of Christ and the resultant biblical truth of their position of being *"in Christ"*. Nevertheless, many Christians persist in the denial of the Scriptural fact of the equally true Biblical fact, that their old life of sin and death, began *"in Adam"*. Read again 1 Cor. 15:22, which explicitly reveals both contexts for men.

> *1 Cor. 15:22 For as **in Adam** <u>all die</u>, even so **in Christ** <u>shall all be made alive.</u>* (If the word "again" would be added to the end of this verse, it would not harm the context,)

A pause is needed here to make a critical distinction in this verse that must be Biblically understood. It is the difference between the two definitions of the two words "all" in 1 Corinthians

15:22. The first "all" is universal in scope, simply because all men are descended from Adam. But the second "all" can, logically, only apply to all of those who are the objects God's fore-ordained election. Why? If the second "all", (*"in Christ"*), was interpreted as being universal in scope, just as the universality of the first "all", (*"in Adam"*), must be, then it would assert universal salvation. Although some people hold the view of universal salvation, it is a position that is Scripturally indefensible. If universal salvation was God's ultimate plan, then all of the Biblical references to Hell, including the revealed truth of Luke 16, about the beggar Lazarus and the rich man, would be an outright lie, or, at the very least, an empty threat.

Condensing the "if-then" Scriptural logic path as revealed in the preceding verses, we find that:

If it is true that:
1. The choice to sin was a God-allowed, free will choice of all men "in Adam" and....
2. The consequence of sin was immediate spiritual death and eventual physical death, and....
3. The fall of man produced a nature in all men that made them "enemies", "alienated", "in bondage", and "dead in sins", towards God, and....
4. Natural (spiritually dead) men cannot receive, nor cannot perceive the "things of the Spirit of God",

Then:
5. The "free will" doctrine, which claims that all unbelievers still have the self-capacity to, and the responsibility to, make their own choice to believe the gospel for salvation, is actually a **"man-made gulf"** which arises from flawed Bible interpretation about the state of mans' fallen nature. The result of this erroneous doctrine is a deception that allows Satan to lead many people to Hell by their pride in

the delusion that they have a "free will", by which they chose to remain in unbelief.

Ever since man's sin in Eden, the doctrine of "presumed free will" has been a myth that degrades the magnitude of God's grace in salvation among believers and a lie that deceives the minds of all unbelievers.

Topic 11. The Fallen Will causes Man's Rejection of God

Despite the "spiritually dead", not just "spiritually ill", condition of all men, Satan will still lead many to Hell by their belief that the salvation decision was theirs' alone to make. There will be many of the "spiritually dead" men who will never hear another direct call to believe beyond the call that they heard "in Adam" in the Garden of Eden, to believe and obey God. Once the initial sin of disbelief occurred in Eden, any future "effectual" salvation calls to mankind were entirely within the divine prerogative of God. The point is affirmed in Exodus and reaffirmed by Paul in Romans.

> *Exo. 33:19 And he said, I will make all my goodness pass before thee, and I will proclaim the name of the LORD before thee; and* **_will be gracious to whom I will be gracious, and will shew mercy on whom I will shew mercy._**
> *Rom. 9:15 For he saith to Moses,* **_I will have mercy on whom I will have mercy, and I will have compassion on whom I will have compassion_**.

The "mercy" and "grace" cited in these verses are displayed by God's "effectual calls" to salvation. But, there will also be "calls" given to other people that will be "ineffectual". These will not be "ineffectual" by any failure on God's part. They will fail because of the blind eyes, deaf ears, and hardened hearts of men that was the result of man's sin in the Garden. Tragically, these conditions of blind eyes, deaf ears and hardened hearts will result in their "putting-off" of their belief decision until a "more convenient time, which they presume they will have.

In such people, the general calls of God, whether through the witness of creation or through an actual physical hearing or reading of the Bible, will fall on blind eyes, deaf ears, and hardened hearts, because of God's divine prerogative in choosing to save "whom He will", by His grace, as cited in Exodus 33:19 and Romans 9:15. The absence of saving grace provided for any person is due to their non-election by God; a secret that only He knows. If saving grace is never given to a person, they will still remain legally responsible for every rejection of whatever calls of God they may experience. Even if their only rejection happened in Eden, it is their "free will' rejection that will seal their condemnation. However, fallen men are naturally biased to continue in their rejection of the various "calls of God".

Here are some Biblical examples of continued, willful rejections by men to "a call of God" scenario:

There was the wealthy man who went so far as to ask the right question. He sought Jesus for eternal life, believing his law obedience would save him. But when Jesus tested the man's heart, he rejected the terms Jesus required.

> *Mar. 10:17 And when he was gone forth into the way, there came one running, and kneeled to him, and asked him, Good Master, **what shall I do that I may inherit eternal life?***

> *Mar. 10:18 And Jesus said unto him, Why callest thou me good? there is none good but one, that is, God.*

Mar. 10:19 Thou knowest the commandments, Do not commit adultery, Do not kill, Do not steal, Do not bear false witness, Defraud not, Honour thy father and mother.

Mar 10:20 And he answered and said unto him, Master, all these (the commandments) *have I observed from my youth.*

*Mar. 10:21 Then Jesus beholding him loved him, and said unto him, One thing thou lackest: go thy way, sell whatsoever thou hast, and give to the poor, and thou shalt have treasure in heaven: and come, take up the cross, and follow me. Mar. 10:22 And **he was sad at that saying, and went away grieved: for he had great possessions**.*

Pontius Pilate, in John 18:38, questioned the "truth" that Jesus offered, but he failed to pursue the answer.

*John 18:37 Pilate therefore said unto him, Art thou a king then? Jesus answered, Thou sayest that I am a king. To this end was I born, and for this cause came I into the world, that I should bear witness unto the truth. **Every one that is of the truth heareth my voice**. John 18:38 **Pilate saith unto him, What is truth?** And when he had said this, he went out again unto the Jews, and saith unto them, I find in him no fault at all.*

Felix, in Acts 24:25, procrastinated for a more "convenient time" to hear the gospel from Paul;

Acts 24:25 And as he (Paul) *reasoned of righteousness, temperance, and judgment to come, **Felix trembled, and answered, Go thy way for this time;***

when I have a convenient season, I will call for thee.

Later, Agrippa, in Acts 26:28, likewise felt "almost persuaded" to believe Paul after hearing his testimony.

> *Acts 26:28 Then Agrippa said unto Paul, **Almost thou persuadest me to be a Christian**.*

How many people will end up in Hell bearing an eternal memory of when they:

- heard and rejected the truth?
- put off their decision for a more "convenient time"?
- were "almost persuaded", but chose to remain in their state of rejection?

It will be their "in bondage" wills that will produce the responses above. Whatever their excuse, their memory of it will be a torture worse than the very eternal flames of Hell.

As Paul traveled and preached the new gospel of grace to both his fellow Jews and to the Gentiles, he repeatedly experienced the same reaction as recorded in Acts 28, when preaching to the Jews in Rome.

> *Acts 28:24 And **some believed** the things which were spoken, and **some believed not**.*

He constantly received two different reactions to the same message. Why?

As a final example of the ultimate rejecter, I offer Judas Iscariot. As a chosen disciple of Jesus, Judas was fully exposed to the earthly ministry of Jesus. As one of the twelve, Judas would have possessed abundant evidence of the miracles, signs, wonders, and teachings that Jesus performed, yet his "will" did not move him to believe in his heart about who Jesus said He was.

The reason for Judas' act of betrayal is revealed by the completed Word of God, which confirms two facts. First, it means Judas did not receive any eye, hear and heart-opening work of God because he was not numbered among those chosen *"before the foundation of the world"* (Eph.1:4). Did Judas know this? No. Second, Judas was not unfairly excluded from saving belief, but rather was left by God, in his state of unbelief (sin) that he, and all men, chose "in Adam". But God did not compel Judas' choice "in Adam". He merely left Judas in his choice. The gift of grace is defined as the receiving of something completely undeserved. Judas did not receive the gift of saving grace. There is no unfairness in not receiving that which one does not deserve. God alone is the distributor of saving grace, which no one deserves.

God then, in the verse below, allowed Satan to use, not force, Judas to betray Jesus. God, in His sovereign prerogative used Judas' sin nature to trigger the foreordained betrayal and crucifixion of Christ (Acts 2:23). The amount of physical evidence about Jesus, as witnessed by Judas, did not dissuade his persistence in his rejection of Jesus. Jesus, in His omniscience, knew that Judas was not among the elect and allowed Satan to take control of him and play his part in fulfilling prophecy. He even commanded Judas to carry out his betrayal - quickly.

> John 13:27 And after the sop *Satan entered into him.* **Then said Jesus unto him, That thou doest, do quickly.**

Each of these "rejection" examples are so typical of the "rejections" people are still using today. Each of the people in the verses above were confronted in some manner with God's truth. But, because of their "in bondage" wills, none were sovereignly enabled to "believe". Nevertheless, all men who die in their state of rejection of God will spend eternity in hell believing that, as" gods" of their own destinies, they could have willfully believed. But, each one will forever know that it was "in Adam" where they made their real "free will" choice not to believe. They will also know that they remained content to adhere to their original choice all their life. No man, who dies in his or her sin, will be able to plead ignorance in Hell. Satan successfully deceived "all men" in the Garden, and will keep millions of men (those not elect of God) deceived on their way to Hell, by using the illusion that they always possessed a "free will choice". The belief that they could have believed was, in reality, what I will label as the "free will gulf".

Furthermore, all the deceived occupants of Hell will never be aware of the spiritual truth of their "non-election" by God. God's sovereign, pre-creation act of election of some to salvation is a *"spiritual thing (truth) of God"*; a thing that cannot be known by any lost man, as 1 Corinthians 2:14 affirms.

> *1 Cor. 2:14 But the <u>natural man</u> **<u>receiveth not</u>** the things of the Spirit of God: for they are foolishness unto him: **<u>neither can he know</u>** them, because they are spiritually discerned.*

Conversely, the essence of, and glory of, the pure grace of God will be fully revealed to all saved persons, when the knowledge of their election is fully comprehended in heaven. Salvation only comes to those whom God chose to save by His will and grace alone. Is being one of God's elect a reason for pride? No, humble and total gratitude is the only possible response.

(If this explanation of God's work of election to salvation has stirred any personal anxiety in the heart of the reader about not being one of God's elect, this stirring itself, is a "call of God" to you. I can only exhort you, person to person, "don't ignore this call." Read 1 Cor. 15:3-4 and Rom. 10:9 and respond to your heart. Whether you are "elect" or not, only God knows.)

Why there is "No Excuse"

How does man's understanding factor into their rejection of God? Scripture can be seen as confusing on this subject. Paul, writing in Romans, reveals a truth of which all mankind is aware. In Romans 1:20, he writes under divine inspiration that all men are internally aware of God and His eternal power and, therefore, are aware and understand that God exists. Every non-elect person will stand without any plea of ignorance before God at their day of judgment.

> *Rom. 1:20 For <u>the invisible things of him</u>* (God) *from the creation of the world are **<u>clearly seen, being understood</u>** by the things that are made,* (all mankind) *even his eternal power and Godhead; so **<u>that they are without excuse:</u>***

But an alert critic may counter with Romans 3:11 that says that there are *"none who understand"*.

> *Rom. 3:11 There is **<u>none that understandeth</u>**, there is none that seeketh after God.*

These two verses appear to make openly contradictory statements about mankind's understanding. All apparent Scripture contradictions must be resolved. This contradiction can be resolved by contextually defining what is universally 'understood". In Romans 1:20, it is the reality of, or the existence of, God, that all understand. In Romans 3:11, it is man's state of total unrighteousness, which, in turn, should cause them to seek the help of the very God they are all aware of, but none do. "Righteousness" (or "unrighteousness") is the context set in Romans 3:10.

> *Rom. 3:10 As it is written,* **There is none righteous, no, not one:**

All such men, who are aware of God, but who fail to understand their unrighteousness and who, furthermore, rejected God's grace, as it was first offered in Eden, will be judged guilty of violating God's law. Whether that law was the first law issued in Eden or the law of whatever gospel was provided to them during their lifetime, every man's guilt is established. The "law" (command) for this dispensation of grace is for men to "believe" the gospel of grace (1 Cor. 15:3-4). People think they can, but they are "unable" (2 Cor. 2:14), apart from God's gift of faith (Eph. 2:8-9).

This is the reason why Paul wrote that all men stand guilty before God under the law unless His grace saves them. The "stopped mouths" of all lost men at their judgment will be their acknowledgment of their guilt. At their judgment, there will not even be any place for the judicial question of, "How do you plead?" There will be no presumption of innocence; only the confirmation of guilt.

> *Rom. 3:19 Now we know that what things soever the law saith, it saith* <u>*to them who are under the law:*</u> *that* **every mouth may be stopped, and all the world may become guilty before God.**

It is known from the Bible that Satan is the instigator of all false theology, by his unrelenting deception in the minds and hearts of men of, "God did not really say...". This was the form of his initial lie behind his question to Eve in the Garden regarding what God said to her. Satan planted the seed of doubt in her mind and he has been sowing the same seed of doubt ever since.

> Gen 3:1 "...And he said unto the woman, <u>**Yea, hath God said,**</u>..."

Satan's character was exposed as "the father of lies" by Jesus. In this dialog between Jesus and the Pharisees, recorded in John 8, there was a debate over who was the Pharisees' spiritual "father". The Pharisees tried to claim God as their father (verse 41), but Jesus refuted their claim and told them who their true father was. This accusation by Jesus, of the unbelieving Pharisees, also applies to all men who "believe not".

> John 8:44 Ye are of <u>**your father the devil**</u>, and the lusts of your father ye will do. He was <u>**a murderer from the beginning, and abode not in the truth**</u>, because there is no truth in him. When he speaketh a lie, he speaketh of his own: <u>for **he is a liar, and the father of it**</u>.

Satan's lie started with Eve, and he has never ceased to employ it among men. Yet, it still begs the question, "Why can't a man believe by his or her own will?" The act of believing the gospel by a presumed free will choice to gain salvation is actually a doctrinal mirage perpetuated by the "free will gulf" which lures men to reject the call of God, for perhaps a "more convenient time". The invisible bondage of the will of lost man is just as unbreakable as the barrier that blocked the gate of the Garden of Eden. Ever since the unbelief in the Garden, all men, from birth, by their fallen nature, reject (disbelieve) the very God of which all men are aware.

Topic 12. Salvation by God's Will Alone

The apostle John, in his gospel, testifies to the fact that salvation is solely dependent upon the will (and work) of God alone. The two verses below do not allow one iota of credit to the will of man for his salvation.

> *John 1:12 But **as many as received him**, to them gave he power to become the sons of God, even to them that believe on his name:*
> *John 1:13 **Which were born**, not of blood, nor of the will of the flesh, nor of the will of man, but **of God**.*

Because of the way the events contained in verses 12 and 13 are sequenced, a false cause and effect connection is suggested. In verse 12, the *"power to become sons of God"* is clearly contingent upon the action of having *"received him"*. The phrase of having *"received him"* is further defined at the end of verse 12 by the addition of the phrase, *"to them that believe on his name"*. This is a legitimate cause and effect connection. It asserts that *"power"* is given to those who *"received him"*, which, in turn, is defined as those who *"believed on his name"*. In verse 12, there is no question that the people under discussion are those who have believed.

But, a flawed connection is often made between verses 12 and 13. In verse 13, some Bible teachers conclude that the condition of those *"which were born"*, is also dependent upon the actions of those who *"received him"* (believed), as introduced in verse 12. There are two possible reasons I can suppose, for this mistaken conclusion. The first reason is positional. The "birth" mentioned in verse 13 is often erroneously made contingent to the "receiving" action of verse 12, merely because verse 13 follows verse 12. The second and more plausible reason for this erroneous connection between verse 12 and verse 13 is that it is the preferred interpretation constructed by Arminian theology to protect and maintain their "free will" view. If the "birth" of verse 13 can be portrayed as a contingent reward to those who "received him", then man's free will belief retains its position as the cause of being *"born"* by God's will.

Putting verses 12 and 13 in the correct context refutes the Arminian interpretation. It is a Biblical fact that the expressions *"received him"*, *"believe on his name"* and "born" (in this context), all denote the act leading to salvation. Verse 13, however, is a distinct revelation from verse 12 in that it introduces new information which explains the reasons "why" and "how" anyone "receives", believes" or is "born", while conversely, it lists three factors that have no role in this "birth".

The revelations contained in verse 13, establish the truth that all of those who *"received him"*, *"believed on his name"* and were *"born"* , were **NOT** "born" by "blood" (genetics), or by "the will of the flesh" (works), or by or "the will of man" (free will). The inescapable truth of verse 13 is that the "cause" of every new birth (salvation) depends exclusively upon the will of God.

Topic 13. The Importance of Sound Doctrine

What is the relationship between a person's salvation and the soundness of the doctrine they believe? Consider the following example of a solid doctrinal position as it relates to salvation. There is an often repeated phrase used by many Bible teachers who understand the distinction of the gospel of the dispensation of grace. They make the following declaration to emphasize the distinction of grace. It is the summary statement that says, "Salvation is the result of faith plus nothing!" It is a true statement if the word "nothing" defines what man can contribute. But this common refrain leaves a deeper truth unspoken. It is deep truth as just shown in John 1:13 which irrefutably points to the lone cause of any "receiving", "believing" or being "born".

The more accurate summary statement about "salvation" should be stated as: "Ultimately, Salvation is the result of "God's will and grace plus nothing!"

Faith is, without question, an essential component of salvation, but the expression "faith plus nothing" does not address the question of, "Where does saving faith come from?" The natural, presumptive answer that men give to this question is, "It must come from the decision of each individual." But, as pointed out in the previous topic, verse 13 of John 1 utterly eliminates man's will as the source of saving faith (being "born").

Regarding sound doctrine and faith, a qualifying point of emphasis is necessary. I do not believe or infer that everyone who subscribes to "free will" doctrine as part of their theology, is not, or cannot, be genuinely (Biblically) saved. Flawed theology may divert a person from a full appreciation of the grace that saved them. It can, and it does, divert unbelievers from a genuine salvation, but it cannot negate (remove) the salvation of anyone who has been Biblically saved. I would not be surprised if a majority of God's elect will enter their heavenly rest believing some amount of flawed theology, myself included. Nevertheless, the continual pursuit of sound Christian doctrine is a worthy goal as Paul wrote to Timothy.

> *1 Tim. 4:13 Till I come, **give attendance to reading, to exhortation, to doctrine.***
>
> *2 Tim. 4:2 Preach the word; be instant in season, out of season; reprove, rebuke, **exhort with** all longsuffering and **doctrine**.*
>
> *2 Tim. 4:3 For the time will come when they will not endure **sound doctrine**; but after their own lusts shall they heap to themselves teachers, having itching ears;*

The era of neglecting sound doctrine, as mentioned in verse 3 above, is gaining strength in many churches today. Sound doctrine is a declining priority in Christendom. Doctrinal teaching has given way to political, social, and Christian psychological preaching. Erroneous doctrine can certainly be used by Satan to divert men from the Bible's revealed path to salvation. But, while sound (perfect) doctrine is a desired goal, 100% doctrinal purity was never God's determinant for anyone's salvation.

Belief in the correct gospel in this dispensation of grace is a non-negotiable requirement for salvation, but doctrinal perfection is not. The truth of God's elective will, about all who are, or will be, saved, will come to pass, regardless of the amount of correct theology a believer learns after their salvation. There is a significant amount of doctrinal error and confusion that permeates Christianity today. However, the salvation of God's ordained elect will be accomplished, despite the growing abundance of flawed doctrine in Christendom.

In heaven, I believe that all of those who have been saved will understand all of the doctrinal errors that they held. I believe that this is the point made in 1 Corinthians 13.

> *1 Cor. 13:9* <u>*For* **we know in part**</u>*, and we prophesy in part.*
> *1 Cor. 13:10* <u>***But when that which is perfect is come***</u>*,* <u>*then that which is in part shall be done away.*</u>
> *1 Cor. 13:11 When I was a child, I spake as a child, I understood as a child, I thought as a child: but when I became a man, I put away childish things.*
> *1 Cor. 13:12* <u>***For now we see through a glass, darkly; but then face to face: now I know in part; but then shall I know even as also I am known***</u>.

Some Biblical scholars and teachers contend that the *"perfect"* of verse 13 is a reference to the completed canon of Scripture.

Their teaching point being that since Scripture has been completed, men now have full knowledge of all of God's revelation. But I submit that the context of verses 9 through 12 are applying the phrase *"that which is perfect"* to the person of Jesus Christ. Remember from the first chapter of John's gospel, that Jesus Christ is fully identified as *"the Word"* (John 1:1).

Although Christians now possess the completed written word of God. the confusion and division that remains within Christianity today is evidence that believers are still not unified over the message they "see" and "hear" in the Scriptures. Despite the indwelling of the Holy Spirit within all believers, Satan is still successful in his ability to distort the written word of God, even among believers. For this reason, I believe that the moment of the verse 10 phrase, *"perfect is come"* is clarified in verse 12 when believers have their *"face to face"* encounter. Who will they be meeting? It will be a *"face to face"* encounter with "the Word", who was *"with God"* and who *"was God"* (John 1:1) – Jesus Christ. Because of this promised meeting with the *"perfect"*, every believer will be able to say, *"now I know in part; but then shall I know even as also I am known. "*

Free will advocates will learn in heaven, if not before, that their salvation was purely an act of God's grace, which quickened and enabled their "spiritually dead" wills to believe the gospel. The portion of the bridge (way) to heaven that they thought was reliant on their willful co- operation, never existed. They will realize that while they are responsible for their sin, their salvation never depended upon them. All saved people will fully know in heaven, that their salvation was a gift received, but never deserved. They will *"fully know"* that this is what the truth of the grace of God is all about; that any presumed "free will" contribution from them was a myth.

Should you think that my opposition to free will theology is excessive, consider again, this verse from 1 Corinthians. If you accept the truth about the spiritual deadness that fell on "all in

Adam", then this verse declares the existence of a "fixed gulf". The inability to *"spiritually discern"*, that prevents all lost men from "effectually hearing" the gospel by their own will is the last "fixed gulf" of this discussion. By the term "effectual hearing", is meant hearing, with heart-opened understanding, the gospel, which leads to the imputation of saving faith within a person. But:

> *1 Cor. 2:14 But the natural man <u>receiveth not the things of the Spirit of God</u>: for they are foolishness unto him: <u>neither **can** he know them, because they are spiritually discerned.</u>*

Regarding salvation, this verse is analogous to my introductory anecdote. It is God (as the farmer) telling the lost man (as the salesman), "Try as you will, you can't get there from here!" (by your own effort, will or intellect). It is a verse of very bad news, "if" that is all there was. But, there is more. The good news unfolds in the rest of Scripture, where it proceeds to tell lost men, that Jesus is the only way, and that only by God's grace can you ever "see" (perceive) that Jesus is the way."

Today, faith in the death, burial, and resurrection of Jesus Christ is the one and only gospel bridge to every lost man's "fixed gulf" problem. Faith, heart-opened belief (Rom 10:9), in this truth is a pure gift of God. While the correct gospel is essential for salvation, growth in sound doctrine will help believers to be *"...a good minister of Jesus Christ"* (1 Tim. 4:6) and will protect believers from*"....every wind of doctrine, by the sleight of men, and cunning craftiness, whereby they lie in wait to deceive; "* (Eph. 4:14)

Topic 14. Salvation in this Age of Grace is a Mystery

There is a passage in 1 Peter that alludes to the special nature of God's gift of salvation. It is a gift that intrigued both the prophets and the angels. Peter was writing to encourage his audience of Jewish believers to endure the tribulations that accompanied their belief because of the glory that awaited them.

> *1 Pet. 1:9 Receiving the end of your faith, even **the salvation of your souls**.*
> *1 Pet. 1:10 **Of which salvation** **the prophets have enquired** and searched diligently, **who prophesied of the grace that should come unto you**:*
> *1 Pet. 1:11 Searching what, or what manner of time the Spirit of Christ which was in them did signify, when it testified beforehand the sufferings of Christ, and the glory that should follow.*
> *1 Pet. 1:12 Unto whom it was revealed, that not unto themselves, but unto us they did minister the things, which are now reported unto you by them that have preached the gospel unto you with the Holy Ghost sent down from heaven; **which things the angels desire to look into**.*

Salvation was such a mystery that even the angels, who had not fallen, as well as the prophets of the Old Testament, desired to know how it would work. Allow me to offer a hypothetical, heavenly conversation of how an inquiry by the angels, to God, might have sounded. (I will borrow, and slightly modify an appropriate answer that comes from a well-known, but worldly movie.) The conversation could have gone something like this:

Angels: "Lord God, we see now that man, made in your image, has fallen captive to Satan by sinning and that you have separated yourself from them by a great gulf fixed." "Lord God, because of this separation, how can any man possibly be redeemed from this condemnation that You have set?"

God: "Fear not. I have already chosen all of whom I will save. I will, in due time, save all of my elect, by *making them an offer they won't refuse.*"

If you are a child of God today, you should be, daily, thanking "God the Father" for making this offer to you; an offer that you could not refuse. He overcame your hard heart of refusal by the opening it to hear His Word, which then freed your captive will to receive His gift of the faith of Jesus, and which, in turn, gave birth to your saving belief (faith). It was by this method of grace alone, through faith alone, that God brought you across the "great fixed gulf" that had separated you from God, culminating in your confession of belief.

The highest truth of this mysterious gift of salvation is that the recipients of it were sovereignly determined from *"before the foundation of the world".* Such salvation should create pure humility in all who are saved. Why? Because when one realizes that he or she was pre-destined to salvation, there are absolutely no remaining grounds for pride. Human pride can only originate from something that man does, or is. Salvation by "pure grace" is the receiving of something that is entirely undeserved. Therefore, the seed of pride should have no ground for germination and growth in the heart of God's elect, once they understand the magnitude of what He has done for them.

But, if the "free will" formula of salvation were true, then at the bare minimum, there would be one justifiable seed of pride found in the heart of everyone who is saved. Their pride would logically arise from the knowledge that their "belief decision" was their's alone. Without their "free-will" compliance in the step of belief, all of God's provisionary work through Jesus and all of God's drawing work on them would be to no avail. This hypothetical would mean that God's salvific drawing work, (*"No man can come to me, except the Father which hath sent me draw him:. John 6:44")* could have failed and that His will might not be done "*among the* "*inhabitants of the earth*" (Dan. 4:35), if man's will was truly free. It would mean that there is some degree of purely independent, human co-operation required for any salvation.

Furthermore, all of God's elective choices could fail to be accomplished if the wills of His elect did not co-operate. The predestinating truth of God's election, as revealed, through Paul, is probably, the hardest truth of all for Christians to understand or accept. But, God has revealed in His Word, the truth of all of the sequential components that accomplish all predestined salvations. Taken as a whole, these components confirm that salvation is truly and wholly "of the Lord", as David testified.

> *Psa. 3:8 __Salvation belongeth unto the LORD__: thy blessing is upon thy people. Selah*

Conclusion

GOD IS SOVEREIGN, IN all of His creation and in the redemption of fallen creation, according to His foreordained will. Although the redemption process appears to be slow in its accomplishment, God's plan is proceeding according to His exact timeline and will. The narrative of Scripture seems to flow erratically, but we are assured in Acts 15 that everthing has, is, and will, continue to run according to His foreordained knowledge and will.

> *Acts 15:18 Known unto God are all his works from the beginning of the world.*

In the course of God's redemptive plan for man and creation, God has put many barriers, that I have labeled as "fixed gulfs", between Himself and man. All of these "gulfs" serve the sovereignty of God's purpose of bringing full glory to Himself through the miracle of salvation. No man can overcome any of God's "fixed gulfs" by his own will or effort alone.

In the pages that followed the discussion of the revelation of the "great gulf fixed" between Hell and Paradise, other occurrences in Scripture were identified where God supernaturally intervened to obstruct any action by the will of man to regain access to Him by the means of a "fixed gulf". While these occurrences are not specifically labeled as "gulfs" in the Bible, they, nevertheless, represent the same insurmountable obstacle to man as does the "great gulf fixed" described in Luke 16:19-31.

Part 2 of this book focused upon a seventh "fixed gulf" that is the most obscure and misunderstood "gulf" in Scripture. A unique distinction of the seventh "gulf" is that, although it was allowed by God, this "gulf" was the product of a prophecy by Satan, given to man in the Garden. The "gulf of presumed free will" has been successfully planted and perpetuated in the mind of fallen humanity by Satan. It is the "gulf" based upon the false doctrine which contends that man's free will is a necessary component of his salvation.

Although listed as the seventh "gulf" in this discussion, the presumption that man's "free will" continued in Adam's descendants, and that it can be used to recover his relationship with God, continued in the mind of man immediately after his disobedience in Eden. By their now corrupted wills, Adam and Eve immediately attempted to remedy their newly perceived nakedness problem by making fig leaf aprons. It failed, as would all of man's subsequent, self-willed efforts to re-establish their relationship with the Creator. To reveal the unrepairable separation that sin created, God proceeded, chronologically, to apply the following "gulfs" upon mankind:

- the locked gate of the Garden of Eden
- the flood and Noah's ark
- the confusion of human language
- the choice of, and promises to, Abraham as the father of a chosen people, to the exclusion of the remainder of humanity
- the giving of the Law to the chosen nation of Israel under the requirement of perfect obedience

The shared distinction of each of these "gulfs" is the fact that any effort by the free will of man could not surmount the separation which God set in place. The unavoidable results of each of the preceding "gulfs" were:

- re-entry to Eden was impossible
- safe passage on the ark was denied to everyone except the eight people chosen by God
- mankind was forced to scatter over the earth by the confusion of human language
- no Gentile had access to promises of God, given to His chosen people through Abraham
- the Law, given to the chosen nation Israel for salvation, exposed the inability of their willful obedience.

Ironically, through the ages of history since the fall in Eden, God always allowed men's repeated "free will" attempts to try to obey and overcome the various "gulfs" that have confronted them. The reason God permitted these attempts was for the ultimate purpose of teaching men that salvation can only come by His will and grace alone. The "fixed gulfs" discussed in Part 1 are readily apparent. But, the reality of a seventh gulf, salvation gained by the "free will" of man, can only be discovered by a rightly divided analysis of the "whole counsel of God".

Today, the first "fixed gulf" created by man's original sin, that has always separated man from God, can only be crossed by grace through the "gift" of faith in the death, burial, and resurrection of Jesus Christ. Any variety of salvation doctrine that requires any degree of merit in a person or any specific works contribution from a person, including a "presumed free will" choice, cannot be defined as a doctrine of salvation by "pure grace". Salvation must be by *"Sola Gratia"* because we became "wretched" and "separated" in Adam. God's sovereignty in salvation is purposely displayed through His employment of the succession of all of His "fixed gulfs".

Grace is the only means of access to the bridge that can provide a crossing of any "fixed gulf" of God. Jesus Christ is the embodiment of all such grace. The salvation of any man, in any era of history was, is, or will be, achieved only by God's grace through the "gift" faith, given "to whom He wills". While the specific gospel message to be believed has been changed by God through the various Biblical dispensation periods, the gift of grace, that is needed for men to believe, has never changed. The salvation sequence was ordained by God – Father, Son and Holy Spirit, before the beginning of creation. All that believers can do is agree with this doxology of Romans 11.

> *Rom. 11:33 O the depth of the riches both of the wisdom and knowledge of God! how unsearchable are his judgments, and his ways past finding out!*
> *Rom. 11:34 For who hath known the mind of the Lord? or who hath been his counsellor?*
> *Rom. 11:35 Or who hath first given to him, and it shall be recompensed unto him again?*
> *Rom. 11:36 For of him, and through him, and to him, are all things: to whom be glory for ever. Amen.*

I thank God for:
1. the lessons of His *"great gulf(s) fixed"*,
2. the truth that I can take no credit for my salvation,
3. "fixing" my "great gulf problem" by bestowing salvation upon me through:

CONCLUSION

The death, burial and resurrection of
Jesus Christ alone,
through the "gift" of faith alone,
by God's grace alone,
and
according to God's fore-ordained will alone.

A Great Gulf Fixed

CONCLUSION